I am in
Your Support
Love.
Amil

Restored, Rescued, and Redeemed by Jesus

# Restored, Rescued, and Redeemed by Jesus

*Seven Minor-Character Vignettes
from the Fourfold Gospel*

## Amir M. Dinkha

RESOURCE *Publications* · Eugene, Oregon

To the beloved memory of my father, Matty Dinkha, whose simple, but profound, faith instilled in me at an early age the curiosity to discover the Jesus of the fourfold Gospel.

To my mother, Maryam Ḥanna, whose presence, unconditional love, and fervent intercessions have continuously brought me immense solace and joy.

I dedicate this work to them as a token of my utmost love, affection, and gratitude.

"For my purposes a 'minor' character is one who lacks a continuing or recurrent presence in the story as narrated. For the most part, minor characters appear only once."

—Elizabeth Struthers Malbon

# Contents

# Preface

THE HISTORICAL FIGURE JESUS, who lived sometime between 6 BCE and 33 CE[1] in the Roman-controlled region of Palestine,[2] wrote nothing at all about himself in his native spoken languages of Aramaic and Hebrew. Yet, at the close of the first century CE, four identical and divergent documents about his life, teaching, work, passion, death, and resurrection, written in Greek, were circulating in the Greco-Roman Mediterranean world. These documents, still extant, have been universally known for almost two millennia as the fourfold Gospel according to Matthew, Mark, Luke, and John. They are, after all, the most important historical Christian source documents concerning Jesus.

The person of Jesus is the most prominent protagonist in the fourfold Gospel narratives. Since he is simply the focal point, everything, from beginning to end, revolves around him directly or obliquely. He is portrayed as the preeminent and unique expression, representation, and embodiment of God's presence in human history. Next to Jesus, the disciples, the crowds, and the religiopolitical authorities and leaders are the major male character groups. They are constantly in view, whether taking the center stage or looming in the background of a particular event. They are woven into the fabric of the overall narrative plot and subplots of each Gospel. They are portrayed as either friendly or hostile to Jesus. In addition, there

1. The abbreviations BCE (Before Common Era) and CE (Common Era) are used throughout this book instead of BC (Before Christ) and AD (Latin: *anno Domini,* "in the year of the Lord").

2. The region of Palestine was known during the course of history by many different names, such as Canaan, Israel, and Judea. Today, it is geopolitically divided between the country of Israel, the Palestinian Authority in the West Bank, and Hamas in the Gaza Strip.

are many minor characters who populate the fourfold Gospel.[3] They exist only as they pass in and out of a literary pericope.[4] They do not play a continuing role within the overall literary flow and context of a Gospel drama, plot, and narrative.

Of the many minor characters in the fourfold Gospel, this book is an attempt to take a closer look at seven of them, who appear suddenly, interact with Jesus briefly, and then vanish quickly. Nevertheless, their presence constitutes an important component of the fourfold Gospel traditions, contribute to the development of the plot of each Gospel, and, inevitably, deepen one's theological understanding of Jesus as God's authoritative and definitive agent of mercy and salvation. These seven minor characters are the woman with the flow of blood (Mark 5:25–34); the blind beggar Bartimaeus (Mark 10:46–52); the gentile centurion at Capernaum (Matt 8:5–13); the sinful woman at the house of Simon the Pharisee (Luke 7:36–50); Zacchaeus, the chief tax collector at Jericho (Luke 19:1–10); the lame man at the pool of Bethesda (John 5:1–18); and the adulterous woman (John 7:53—8:11).

A cursory reading of the seven pericopae comprising this book suffices to show that the seven minor characters share certain traits, such as:

1. *Individuality.* Each one of the seven minor characters stands alone as a realistic and unique individual who does not belong to a wider or larger distinct character group within the world of a Gospel narrative. In other words, each one of them interacts with Jesus individually.

2. *Anonymity.* The reader may find it puzzling that, of the seven minor characters, five surprisingly lack a proper name, and their personal identity remains obscure in the narrative. How should one assess this tendency to anonymity? It seems fair to say that only those minor characters who were known to, or became members of, the early Christian community are distinguished by name, such as Bartimaeus and Zacchaeus.

3. Think of some minor characters such as the leper (Mark 1:40), the poor widow (Mark 12:42), Simon of Cyrene (Mark 15:21), Joseph of Arimathea (Mark 15:43), Caiaphas (Matt 26:57), Pilate's wife (Matt 27:19), Zechariah (Luke 1:5), Elizabeth (Luke 1:5), Simon (Luke 2:25), Anna (Luke 2:36), Mary Magdalene (Luke 8:2), Cleopas (Luke 24:18), and the Samaritan woman (John 4:7).

4. The English word pericope (plural: pericopae) comes from the Greek words περί (*peri*, "around") and κοπή (*kopé*, "cutting"). Thus, a περικοπή (*perikopé*, pericope, "cutting around"), as a term used by scholars, is mostly a self-contained piece, cut out of a Gospel context and, consequently, can stand on its own as an individual literary unit.

3. *Scarcity*. Little is known about each of the seven minor characters, and some of the details seem to be lacking. How long was Bartimaeus blind? Did Zacchaeus continue working as a chief tax collector after his conversion? In addition to anonymity, was the woman with the flow of blood single, married, divorced, or widowed? The scarcity of narrative information may apparently be due to the brevity and momentary appearance of these minor characters on stage.

4. *Personality*. Some minor characters are tight-lipped or laconic, such as the woman with the flow of blood, the sinful woman, Zacchaeus, and the adulteress, while Bartimaeus, the gentile centurion, and the lame man are chatty or loquacious.

Most significantly, these seven pericopae are brief, well-rounded, and complete units, preserved by the Gospel evangelists as an indelible and important constituent of the Jesus traditions. Each one of them may be viewed as a "little gospel"[5] because it offers a glimpse into Jesus' identity and his multifaceted charismatic ministry. The reader will definitely notice that it is Jesus who has the last word in all of these pericopae. As God's authoritative and definitive agent of mercy and salvation, Jesus is depicted in these seven pericopae as a healer, debater, teacher, forgiver, storyteller, prophet, interpreter, and reconciler. Take, for example, Luke 7:36–50. Jesus is portrayed, above all, as a quintessential prophet who extends forgiveness to the sinful woman and, consequently, restores her to communion with God.

The overarching theme of this book is about restoration, rescue, and redemption, both physically and spiritually. The seven minor characters encounter Jesus in a variety of settings and circumstances. As a result of their personal encounter with him, their lives, as well as the lives of their loved ones, are dramatically changed. Jesus compassionately sets them free from their physical suffering, sinful condition, and the fear of social ostracism. This is, of course, particularly true and obvious in the case of Zacchaeus, whose encounter with Jesus leads to the conversion of his whole family. Indeed, the same notion of perspicuity can be extended to the gentile centurion who asks Jesus for the healing of his ailing servant.

The main objective of this book is to offer interpretive insights on each of the seven pericopae. The author does not claim to give an exhaustive coverage of each pericope. Each chapter begins with an English translation of the Greek text of a pericope, taken from the NRSV of the Bible. The reader is

---

5. Strauss, *Four Portraits*, 59.

encouraged to spend a good amount of time slowly and thoughtfully reading each Gospel pericope to uncover and discover its genuine subtlety, beauty, and originality. Where the Greek text is cited, the source is the *GNT* (UBS). The Greek text is also transliterated and translated into English to further enable the reader to understand some nuances that may be missed in the English translation of a pericope. Unless otherwise stated, all Gospel translations from the Greek are the author's own. Then, each chapter is further divided into three interrelated parts. The first part—scholarly context—briefly explores an overview of scholarly interpretations of each pericope. The second part—literary genre and structure—identifies a form-critical category into which a pericope can broadly fall. It also offers a proposed structure, which traces the flow and progression of the plot within each pericope. The third part—narrative analysis—examines each pericope according to its own merits, and views it within the larger Gospel narrative by means of succinctly analyzing how certain elements (i.e., setting, characters, point of view, theme development, conflict, and resolution) interact with each other to form a coherent story, which the omniscient narrator, covertly or overtly, then uses to invite the reader to take sides or to identify with certain values and meanings expressed in each pericope.

Each chapter stands alone on its own merit. It can be almost read independently of others. It is, however, recommended that every chapter is read in connection with what precedes or follows it. For example, the first two chapters in this book, covering pericopae from Mark's Gospel, deserve to be read together to better understand the evangelist's portrait of Jesus. The only exception is chapter 3, dealing with a pericope from Matthew's Gospel. As the reader moves from one chapter to another, he or she will notice a certain amount of unavoidable repetition, for which the author apologizes. It is, however, the author's desire that as you continue reading each chapter of this book, you gradually come to realize the greatness of the Jesus of the fourfold Gospel, whose ultimate mission is to bring and give life in abundance (John 10:10).

# Acknowledgments

THERE ARE MANY PEOPLE I would wholeheartedly like to acknowledge for being such a tremendous help in making this book come to fruition.

This book has evolved over a long period of time from materials presented and taught, albeit in a simplified form, to my students at St. Genevieve High School in Panorama City, Los Angeles. As always, I am thankful to all of my students, whose class discussions have made invaluable contributions to my thinking about each chapter of this book.

I would like to thank Ms. Mary Ann Navarro, a library assistant at St. John's Seminary Libraries in Camarillo, California, for assisting me with finding books and allowing me to make photocopies of a multitude of topics.

I am indebted to Mrs. Linda Jackson, a colleague, friend, and English department chair at St. Genevieve High School, for kindly proofreading the first draft of each chapter and making numerous suggestions on the improvement of my style of writing.

I am grateful to Fr. Ciarán O'Callaghan, CSsR, for reading the first three chapters of the manuscript and offering valuable constructive feedback, particularly for my translations of New Testament Greek.

I would like to express my gratitude to Mr. Matthew Wimer, Editorial Production Manager at Wipf and Stock, for patiently and astutely guiding me through the editing and publishing process.

Above all, I owe my deepest debt of gratitude to Ms. Cecilia Olaguez for her unwavering support and encouragement, particularly during the course of writing this book, as well as for her painstaking attention to the accuracy and consistency of the footnotes and bibliography.

Should you find mistakes, errors, and oversights in this book, please be assured that they are obviously mine alone.

# Abbreviations

## Periodicals, Reference Works, and Serials

| | |
|---|---|
| א | Codex Sinaiticus |
| A | Codex Alexandrinus |
| *ABD* | *The Anchor Bible Dictionary.* Edited by David Noel. Freedman. 6 vols. New York: Doubleday, 1992 |
| B | Codex Vaticanus |
| *BA* | *Biblical Archaeologist* |
| *BDAG* | Walter Bauer et al. *Greek-English Lexicon of the New Testament and Other Early Christian Literature.* 3rd edition. Chicago: University of Chicago Press, 2000 |
| *BDB* | Francis Brown et al. *Hebrew and English Lexicon of the Old Testament with an Appendix Containing the Biblical Aramaic.* 5th printing edition. Peabody, MA: Hendrickson, 2000 |
| *Bib* | *Biblica* |
| C | Codex Ephraemi Rescriptus |
| *CBQ* | *Catholic Biblical Quarterly* |
| *CBR* | *Currents in Biblical Research* |
| CSB | Christian Standard Bible |
| D | Codex Bezae Cantabrigiensis |
| *EvQ* | *Evangelical Quarterly* |

| | |
|---|---|
| *ExpTim* | *Expository Times* |
| *f*1 | Family 1 manuscripts |
| *f*13 | Family 13 manuscripts |
| *GNT* | *The Greek New Testament*. Edited by B. Aland et al. 4th revised edition. Stuttgart: Deutsche Bibelgesellschaft/United Bible Societies, 1993 |
| *HTR* | *Harvard Theological Review* |
| *HvTSt* | *Hervormde teologiese studies* |
| JB | The Jerusalem Bible |
| *JBL* | *Journal of Biblical Literature* |
| *JP* | *Jerusalem Perspective* |
| *JQR* | *Jewish Quarterly Review* |
| *JRE* | *Journal of Religious Ethics* |
| *JSNT* | *Journal for the Study of the New Testament* |
| KJV | King James Version of the Bible |
| "L" | Lukan special material |
| LXX | Septuagint (Greek version of the Hebrew Bible/Old Testament) |
| "M" | Matthean special material |
| MT | Masoretic Text (of the Hebrew Bible/Old Testament) |
| NASB | New American Standard Bible |
| NIV | New International Version of the Bible |
| *NJBC* | *The New Jerome Biblical Commentary*. Edited by Raymond E. Brown et al. 2nd edition Englewood Cliffs, NJ: Prentice-Hall, 2000 |
| *NovT* | *Novum Testamentum* |
| NRSV | New Revised Standard Version of the Bible |
| *NTS* | *New Testament Studies* |
| P66 | Papyrus 66 |

| | |
|---|---|
| P75 | Papyrus 75 |
| Q | Qumran cave manuscripts |
| "Q" | Quelle (Sayings Source for the Gospels of Matthew and Luke) |
| *RB* | *Revue biblique* |
| RSV | Revised Standard Version of the Bible |
| Sem | Semeia |
| TDNT | *Theological Dictionary of the New Testament.* Edited by Gerhard Kittel and Gerhard Friedrich. Translated by Geoffrey W. Bromiley. 10 vols. Grand Rapids: Eerdmans, 1964–1976 |
| Vulg. | Vulgate (common Latin version of the Bible) |
| W | Codex Washington |

## Hebrew Bible/Old Testament

| | |
|---|---|
| Gen | Genesis |
| Exod | Exodus |
| Lev | Leviticus |
| Num | Numbers |
| Deut | Deuteronomy |
| Josh | Joshua |
| Judg | Judges |
| 1 Sam | 1 Samuel |
| 2 Sam | 2 Samuel |
| 1 Kgs | 1 Kings |
| 2 Kgs | 2 Kings |
| Ezra | Ezra |
| Neh | Nehemiah |
| Esth | Esther |

| | |
|---|---|
| Ps (pl. Pss) | Psalms |
| Prov | Proverbs |
| Isa | Isaiah |
| Jer | Jeremiah |
| Ezek | Ezekiel |
| Dan | Daniel |
| Amos | Amos |
| Mic | Micah |
| Zech | Zechariah |

## Hebrew Bible/Old Testament Apocrypha and Pseudepigrapha

| | |
|---|---|
| Tob | Tobit |
| Jdt | Judith |
| Wis | Wisdom of Solomon |
| Sir | Sirach/Ecclesiasticus |
| Sus | Susanna |
| 1 Macc | 1 Maccabees |
| 2 Macc | 2 Maccabees |
| 2 Esd | 2 Esdras |
| 1 En. | 1 Enoch |
| L.A.B. | Liber Antiquitatum Biblicarum (Pseudo-Philo) |
| Pss. Sol. | Psalms of Solomon |
| T. Sol. | Testament of Solomon |

## New Testament

| | |
|---|---|
| Matt | Matthew |
| Mark | Mark |

| | |
|---|---|
| Luke | Luke |
| John | John |
| Acts | Acts of the Apostles |
| Rom | Romans |
| 1 Cor | 1 Corinthians |
| 2 Cor | 2 Corinthians |
| Gal | Galatians |
| Eph | Ephesians |
| Phil | Philippians |
| Col | Colossians |
| 1 Thess | 1 Thessalonians |
| 1 Tim | 1 Timothy |
| 2 Tim | 2 Timothy |
| Heb | Hebrews |
| Jas | James |
| Rev | Revelation |

## New Testament Apocrypha and Pseudepigrapha

| | |
|---|---|
| *Gos. Nic.* | *Gospel of Nicodemus* |
| *Ps.-Clem. Hom.* | *Pseudo-Clementine Homilies* |
| *Ps.-Clem. Rec.* | *Pseudo-Clementine Recognitions* |

## Dead Sea Scrolls

| | |
|---|---|
| 1QSa | The Messianic Rule |
| 3Q15 | The Copper Scroll |
| 4Q252 | Genesis Commentaries |
| 4Q266 | Damascus Document manuscripts |

| 4Q398 | Some Observances of the Law (MMT C) |
| 4Q504 | The Words of Heavenly Lights |
| 4Q521 | A Messianic Apocalypse |
| 11QapPsa | Apocryphal Psalms |
| 11Q19 | The Temple Scroll |

## Greco-Roman Writings

| *Ag. Ap.* | Josephus, *Against Apion* |
| *Alleg. Interp.* | Philo, *Allegorical Interpretation* |
| *Ann.* | Tacitus, *Annals* |
| *Ant.* | Josephus, *Jewish Antiquities* |
| *Cherubim* | Philo, *On the Cherubim* |
| *Hist.* | Tacitus, *History* |
| *J.W.* | Josephus, *Jewish War* |
| *Life* | Josephus, *The Life* |
| *Nat.* | Pliny the Elder, *Natural History* |
| *Od.* | Homer, *Odyssey* |

## Mishnah and Talmud Writings

| *b. ʿAbod. Zar.* | Babylonian Talmud, ʿ*Abodah Zarah* (*Avodah Zarah*) |
| *b. Ber.* | Babylonian Talmud, *Berakot* (*Berakhot*) |
| *b. Šabb.* | Babylonian Talmud, *Šabbat* (*Shabbat*) |
| *b. Sanh.* | Babylonian Talmud, *Sanhedrin* |
| *b. Yoma* | Babylonian Talmud, *Yoma* |
| *m. ʾOhal.* | Mishnah *ʾOhalot* (*Ohalot*) |
| *m. Qidd.* | Mishnah *Qiddušin* (*Qiddushin*) |
| *m. Šabb.* | Mishnah *Šabbat* (*Shabbat*) |

## Christian Writings

| | |
|---|---|
| *Apol. Hier.* | Rufinus, *Apology against Jerome* |
| *Comm. Eccl.* | Didymus, *Commentary on Ecclesiastes* |
| *Did. apost.* | Anonymous, *Didascalia Apostolorum* |
| *Ep. III* | Pacian, *Letter 3 to Sympronian* |
| *Ep. XXV* | Ambrose, *Letter 25 to Studius* |
| *Ep. XXVI* | Ambrose, *Letter 26 to Studius/Irenaeus* |
| *Hist. eccl.* | Eusebius, *History of the Church* |
| *Incomp. nupt.* | Augustine, *Adulterous Marriages* |
| *Pelag.* | Jerome, *Against Pelagius* |
| *Tract. Ev. Jo.* | Augustine, *Tractate on the Gospel of John* |

# 1

# "Who Touched My Garments?"

## Text

25 Now there was a woman who had been suffering from hemorrhages for twelve years. 26 She had endured much under many physicians, and had spent all that she had; and she was no better, but rather grew worse. 27 She had heard about Jesus, and came up behind him in the crowd and touched his cloak, 28 for she said, "If I but touch his clothes, I will be made well." 29 Immediately her hemorrhage stopped; and she felt in her body that she was healed of her disease. 30 Immediately aware that power had gone forth from him, Jesus turned about in the crowd and said, "Who touched my clothes?" 31 And his disciples said to him, "You see the crowd pressing in on you; how can you say, 'Who touched me?'" 32 He looked all around to see who had done it. 33 But the woman, knowing what had happened to her, came in fear and trembling, fell down before him, and told him the whole truth. 34 He said to her, "Daughter, your faith has made you well; go in peace, and be healed of your disease."

Mark 5:25–34 (NRSV)[1]
(See also Matt 9:20–22; Luke 8:43–48)

## Scholarly Context

THE GREAT MAJORITY OF New Testament scholars accept the basic premises of the Two-Document Hypothesis, which basically asserts the priority of the Gospel of Mark and the posteriority of the Gospels of Matthew and Luke. This simply means that Mark was chronologically the earliest Gospel

1. Each pericope in this book is assigned to a particular Sunday or weekday in the Catholic Lectionary for Mass. The pericope of Mark 5:25–34, or Mark 5:21–43, is liturgically read on the thirteenth Sunday of Ordinary Time, Cycle B. I wish to thank Fr. Felix Just, SJ, for his assistance with this matter.

to have been written in Greek, probably between 67–70 CE, and that the evangelists Matthew and Luke used it as one of their primary sources independently of each other.[2] As a result, the Markan passages, which have parallels in the Gospels of Matthew and Luke, are often referred to by scholars as the Triple Tradition (e.g., Mark 4:35–41 || Matt 8:23–27 || Luke 8:22–25; Mark 9:2–8 || Matt 17:1–8 || Luke 9:28–36; Mark 10:17–31 || Matt 19:16–30 || Luke 18:18–30; Mark 12:13–17 || Matt 22:15–22 || Luke 20:20–26). The present pericope of the woman with the flow of blood, found in all three Synoptic Gospels, qualifies as a Triple-Tradition story (Mark 5:25–34 || Matt 9:20–22 || Luke 8:43–48).

The pericope of the woman with the flow of blood, as found in Mark 5:25–34, is quite unique. It is the only healing-miracle story intercalated or woven into the middle of two halves of another miracle, viz., the pericope of the resuscitation of Jairus's little daughter (Mark 5:21–24, 35–43). How should one explain this phenomenon adequately? There has been an ongoing scholarly debate over whether this intercalation, colloquially known as the sandwich technique, literally reflects original reality and occurrence,[3] or is purely a compositional literary device,[4] either developed in the pre-Markan tradition,[5] or invented by the evangelist Mark himself.[6]

It is fitting, however, to briefly mention that there exist some stylistic differences between the two intercalated pericopae in Mark 5:21–43. Whereas the pericope of Jairus's little daughter (Mark 5:21–24, 35–43) mainly uses the imperfect and historical present tenses, is written with short sentences, and has a few participles, the pericope of the woman with the flow of blood (Mark 5:25–34) mostly utilizes the aorist tense and consists of long, participle-filled sentences.[7] This may point to the fact that they may have originally

---

2. On the literary relationship between the Synoptic Gospels—Mark, Matthew, and Luke—see further Neirynck, "Synoptic Problem," 587–95; Tuckett, "Synoptic Problem," 263–70.

3. See Taylor, *Gospel According to St. Mark*, 289; Cranfield, *Gospel According to St. Mark*, 182.

4. See Shepherd, "Narrative Function," 523; Dewey, *Markan Public Debate*, 22.

5. See Dibelius, *From Tradition to Gospel*, 219; Bultmann, *History of the Synoptic Tradition*, 214; Donahue, *Are You the Christ?*, 59.

6. See Schweizer, *Good News According to Mark*, 116; Achtemeier, *Mark*, 31; Achtemeier, *Jesus and the Miracle Tradition*, 71; Hooker, *Commentary on the Gospel According to St. Mark*, 147.

7. See Achtemeier, "Toward the Isolation," 277; Guelich, *Mark 1—8:26*, 292; Meier, *Marginal Jew*, 2:708–9; Marcus, *Mark 1–8*, 364; Edwards, *Gospel According to Mark*, 160; Stein, *Mark*, 262; Moloney, *Gospel of Mark*, 109; Focant, *Gospel According to Mark*, 216.

been two independent, complete, separate, and self-contained units of oral tradition, intercalated together either by the evangelist or at some time in the tradition before him. Paul J. Achtemeier even suggests that in the written *Vorlage* used by the evangelist the pericope of the woman with the flow of blood originally preceded the pericope of the resuscitation of Jairus's little daughter, and that Mark redactionally inserted the former into the latter, creating a space within the intercalated pericopae.[8]

It is obvious that intercalations are predominantly characteristic of Mark's Gospel, which contains, as Frans Neirynck points out, at least six major intercalations: (1) Mark 3:20–21 [22–30] 31–35; (2) Mark 5:21–24 [25–34] 35–43; (3) Mark 6:7–13 [14–29] 30; (4) Mark 11:12–14 [15–19] 20–25; (5) Mark 14:1–2 [3–9] 10–11; and (6) Mark 14:53–54 [55–65] 66–72.[9] Intriguingly enough, of these six major Markan intercalations, the evangelists Matthew and Luke only retain and preserve the intercalated structure of the two pericopae of Mark 5:21–24 [25–34] 35–43 (Matt 9:18–19 [20–22] 23–26; Luke 8:40–42 [43–48] 49–56). Noticeably, the Matthean and Lukan accounts of the pericope of the woman with the flow of blood are stylistically terse than that of Mark. For instance, whereas the Greek text of Mark 5:25–34 has 154 words, Matthew 9:20–22 has forty-eight words and Luke 8:43–48 has 105 words. It is better, according to Vernon K. Robbins, to describe the literary dependence of Matthew 9:20–22 and Luke 8:43–48 on Mark 5:25–34 as rhetorical rather than scribal. Each of the three Synoptic accounts, therefore, has a different perspective and emphasis. In telling the story of the woman with the flow of blood, Mark's Gospel, for example, focuses on actions, inner perceptions, and emotions.[10]

It is, of course, possible that the answer to the question of why the two pericopae of the woman with the flow of blood and the resuscitation of Jairus's little daughter are found intercalated may actually lie within their thematic similarities and differences. In terms of similarities, both deal with (1) female patients (Mark 5:23, 25); (2) who are anonymous minor characters; (3) considered ritually impure (Mark 5:23, 25); (4) associated with the number "twelve years" (Mark 5:25, 42); (5) called "daughter" (Mark 5:23, 34); (6) healed through physical contact with Jesus (Mark 5:23, 27, 41); and (7) restored to family, community, fertility, and sexuality. In terms of differences, (1) the little daughter has her father pleading her

8. See Achtemeier, *Jesus and the Miracle Tradition*, 70–71.

9. See Neirynck, *Duality in Mark*, 133.

10. See Robbins, "Woman Who Touched," 502–15.

cause to Jesus (Mark 5:23), whereas the woman with the flow of blood has no advocate; and (2) the resuscitation of Jairus's little daughter occurs in a private space, viz., in a room, while the healing of the woman with the flow of blood happens in a public place, viz., on the road.

One may also wonder whether the juxtaposition between the two minor characters—Jairus and the woman with the flow of blood—may also have caused the two pericopae to be intercalated. As one of the leaders of the synagogue, Jairus has a name and is a man of some stature, holding a position of authority and respect in the socioreligious life of the Jewish community, whereas the woman with the flow of blood is anonymous and identified by her affliction. Jairus sees Jesus (ἰδὼν, *idōn*, "having seen," Mark 5:22), while the woman with the flow of blood hears about Jesus (ἀκούσασα, *akousasa*, "having heard," Mark 5:27). Furthermore, the behavior of both minor characters conveys a stark contrast. For instance, both characters fall directly before Jesus, an action indicating entreaty or submission (Mark 5:22, 34); although Jairus πίπτει (*piptei*, "falls down," Mark 5:22) at the feet of Jesus before the healing of his little daughter (note the use of the verb in the historical present tense), the woman with the flow of blood προσέπεσεν (*prosepesen*, "fell down before," Mark 5:33) Jesus after her miraculous healing (note the use of the verb in the aorist tense).

One also needs to keep in mind that the purpose of intercalating one pericope within another in an A1-B-A2 schema is always interpretive and interactive in the context of Mark's narrative.[11] Consequently, the outer pericope of the resuscitation of Jairus's little daughter (A1 = Mark 5:21–24; A2 = Mark 5:35–43) is to be theologically understood by, and thematically juxtaposed and contrasted with, the inner pericope of the woman with the flow of blood (B = Mark 5:25–34) and vice versa. The end result is a single, coherent, and inseparable unit that forms an integral and intimate entity. Take into consideration the fact that the healing of the woman with the flow of blood results in a tormenting delay, which in turn provides a time-lapse during which Jairus's little daughter, who is near death in Mark 5:23, actually dies in Mark 5:35.[12] Furthermore, the two intercalated pericopae undeniably demonstrate Jesus' power over elements of life, viz., disease in the case of the woman with the flow of blood, and death in the case of Jairus's little

11. See Edwards, "Markan Sandwiches," 196; Edwards, *Gospel According to Mark*, 160; Malbon, *In the Company of Jesus*, 26–27.

12. See Dibelius, *From Tradition to Gospel*, 72; Bultmann, *History of the Synoptic Tradition*, 214.

daughter. They both unequivocally highlight, as Christopher D. Marshall points out, the motif of faith as the governing theme in receiving the divine, miraculous power of God's activity in Jesus (Mark 5:34, 36).[13]

## Literary Genre and Structure

In terms of literary genre, the pericope of the woman with the flow of blood falls neatly into the category of healing-miracle stories "in which no struggle takes place but the healing is brought about by the transference of a miraculous energy from the miracle-worker to the sick person."[14] It clearly follows the basic threefold pattern common to all such miracles. First, the *description of disease* contains a brief diagnosis of the patient's illness: the woman suffers from a twelve-year-long, incurable blood-related affliction (Mark 5:25–26). Second, the *healing of disease* shows that the patient's illness is solely rectified by a miracle-worker: the woman with the flow of blood is healed from her twelve-year-long, incurable affliction after touching Jesus' garment (Mark 5:27c–28). Third, the *proof of healing* provides at least some evidence, which confirms the success of the miracle itself: the woman with the flow of blood experiences the healing of her body, and she tells Jesus the whole truth (Mark 5:29, 33).

Within the typical threefold pattern of a healing-miracle story lies a number of recurring motifs characteristic of ancient Jewish, Hellenistic, and Greco-Roman healing-miracle stories. These motifs have been listed by scholars such as Rudolf Bultmann,[15] Hendrik van der Loos,[16] and Barry Blackburn.[17] Relying now on the catalogue of the thirty-three motifs provided by Gerd Theissen,[18] it is possible to detect at least fifteen literary motifs in the pericope of the woman with the flow of blood. They include:

1. The Coming of the Miracle-Worker ("And Jesus having again crossed over in the boat to the other side," Mark 5:21).

2. The Appearance of the Crowd (". . . a great crowd," Mark 5:21, 24; ". . . in the crowd," Mark 5:27; ". . . the crowd," Mark 5:31).

---

13. See Marshall, *Faith as a Theme*, 101.
14. Theissen and Merz, *Historical Jesus*, 293.
15. See further Bultmann, *History of the Synoptic Tradition*, 220–26.
16. See further Loos, *Miracles of Jesus*, 120–30.
17. See further Blackburn, *Theios Anēr*, 200–32.
18. See Theissen, *Miracle Stories*, 47–72; Theissen and Merz, *Historical Jesus*, 283–85.

3. The Appearance of the Distressed Person (". . . and a woman," Mark 5:25; ". . . having come up," Mark 5:27; ". . . [she] came," Mark 5:33).

4. Reasons Given for the Appearance of the "Opposite Numbers" (". . . having heard concerning Jesus," Mark 5:27).

5. Description of the Distress (". . . being in a flow of blood twelve years, and having suffered much under many physicians, and having spent all of her things, and having benefited in no way, but having come into the worse," Mark 5:25–26).

6. Difficulties in the Approach ("And a great crowd was accompanying him and pressing upon him," Mark 5:24).

7. Falling to the Knees (". . . and [she] fell down before him," Mark 5:33).

8. Pleas and Expressions of Trust ("If I even touch his garments, I shall be saved," Mark 5:28).

9. Misunderstanding ("You see the crowd pressing upon you, and you say, 'Who touched me?,'" Mark 5:31).

10. Assurance ("Daughter, your faith has saved you," Mark 5:34; ". . . and be healthy from your affliction," Mark 5:34).

11. Touch (". . . [she] touched his garment," Mark 5:27; "If I even touch his garments," Mark 5:28; "Who touched my garments," Mark 5:30; "Who touched me?," Mark 5:31).

12. Healing Substances (". . . power having gone forth out of him," Mark 5:30).

13. Recognition of the Miracle (". . . and immediately the fountain of her blood was dried up," Mark 5:29).

14. Demonstration (". . . and she knew in the body that she was cured from the affliction," Mark 5:29).

15. Dismissal (". . . go into peace/go in peace," Mark 5:34).

As to literary structure, the pericope of the woman with the flow of blood consists of four scenes: (1) introduction and description (Mark 5:25–26), (2) action and immediacy of healing (Mark 5:27–29), (3) dialogue between Jesus and disciples (Mark 5:30–32), and (4) posthealing encounter (Mark 5:33–34).

## Narrative Analysis

### Introduction and Description
### (Mark 5:25–26)

After the exorcism of the Gerasene demoniac (Mark 5:1–20), Jesus sails back with his disciples from the eastern gentile shore to the western Jewish shore of the Sea of Galilee, also known today as Lake Tiberias and Lake Kinneret. Once ashore, he is met by a large crowd. Jairus, a synagogue ruler, approaches him and begs him to come to his house and lay hands on his dying little daughter so as to heal or, better to say, save her. Jesus goes with him. A large crowd accompanies Jesus and jostles him (Mark 5:21–24). It is at this moment that the flow and thread of the pericope of Jairus's little daughter is interrupted by the immediate introduction of the pericope of the woman with the flow of blood (Mark 5:25–34).

While Jesus is *en route* to Jairus's house, a new character appears on the scene: καὶ γυνὴ οὖσα ἐν ῥύσει αἵματος δώδεκα ἔτη (*kai gynē ousa en rhysei haimatos dōdeka etē*, "and a woman being in a flow of blood twelve years," Mark 5:25). This Markan laconic description sets the stage for the unfolding of the pericope. It moreover underlines three important facts about the female minor character: anonymity, type of the physical illness, and length of the disease. First, the woman is anonymous,[19] just like so many of the women who pass through Mark's Gospel nameless, such as the mother-in-law of Simon Peter (Mark 1:29–31), the daughter of Jairus (Mark 5:21–24, 35–43), the Syrophoenician woman, as well as her daughter (Mark 7:24–30), the poor widow (Mark 12:41–44), and the woman at Bethany (Mark 14:3–9). However, there is certainly a slight difference between these women. The mother-in-law of Simon Peter, the daughter of Jairus, the woman with the flow of blood, and the daughter of the Syrophoenician woman are direct recipients of Jesus' healing power, whereas the Syrophoenician woman, the poor widow, and the woman at Bethany are not.

---

19. Eusebius (*Hist. eccl.* 7:18), a fourth-century church historian, mentions that he visited the house of the woman with the flow of blood, which was located in the city of Caesarea Philippi (Paneas, now Banias, situated on the foothills of Mount Hermon), and saw a bronze statue of a woman kneeling, with her hands stretched out (a representation of the woman with the flow of blood), and another upright bronze statue of a man extending his hand toward the woman (a depiction of Jesus). According to the apocryphal Gospel of Nicodemus, also called Acts of Pilate, a mid-fourth-century document, the woman with the flow of blood is given the name of Bernice/Veronica (*Gos. Nic.* 7:1).

Second, the exact diagnosis of the medical condition of the woman with the flow of blood is unspecified. However, because the two Markan statements οὖσα ἐν ῥύσει αἵματος (*ousa en rhysei haimatos*, "being in a flow of blood," Mark 5:25) and ἡ πηγὴ τοῦ αἵματος αὐτῆς (*hē pēgē tou haimatos autēs*, "the fountain of her blood," Mark 5:29) are employed in the LXX of Leviticus (Lev 12:7; 15:19, 25; 20:18) when talking about a woman's normal menstrual flow and abnormal discharges beyond menstruation, scholars speculate that, in all likelihood, the woman in this pericope might have suffered, as John R. Donahue and Daniel J. Harrington point out, from some chronic vaginal bleeding.[20] John P. Meier, however, thinks that the woman's gynecological problem is "perhaps chronic uterine hemorrhage."[21] Either way, the woman would be technically described, in Jewish terms, not as a נִדָּה (*niddāh*, a woman who produces vaginal blood during her regular menstrual period[22]) but as a זָבָה (*zābāh*, a woman who produces vaginal blood not during her regular menstrual period[23]).[24]

Third, the length of time of the disease, viz., twelve years, undoubtedly highlights the drastic condition of the incurable affliction of the woman with the flow of blood. There is no need to interpret the number twelve years symbolically.[25] It merely functions to evoke sympathy and empathy in the reader/listener for the woman with the flow of blood who is quite hopeless and helpless. The reference to the duration of disease, sickness, or illness is a typical feature of miracle stories (e.g., Luke 13:11 [eighteen years]; John 5:5 [thirty-eight years]; Acts 9:33 [eight years]). Occasionally, the phrase, "from birth," is employed (e.g., John 9:1; Acts 3:2).

The woman's acute gynecological problem would have taken an enormous toll on every aspect of her entire life. As a זָבָה (*zābāh*), she would have been experiencing excruciating pain, ritually considered impure (Lev 12:2), sexually unavailable all the days of the discharge (Lev 18:19; *Ant.* 3.12.1 §275), presumably divorced since every sexual intimacy with her husband would have rendered him impure for seven days (Lev 15:24; having intercourse with a menstruant is an abominable deed according to

20. See Donahue and Harrington, *Gospel of Mark*, 180.

21. Meier, *Marginal Jew*, 2:709. For further information on this issue, see Derrett, "Mark's Technique," 474–505.

22. See *BDB*, 622.

23. See *BDB*, 264.

24. See further Neusner, "Religious Meaning," 3:67–91; Marcus, *Mark 1–8*, 357.

25. See Collins, *Mark*, 280; Stein, *Mark*, 267.

Ezek 22:10),[26] incapable of conceiving and bearing children (*Nat.* 7.13), religiously restricted from participating in Jerusalem Temple worship and forbidden from entering Qumranite sanctuary (*J.W.* 5.5.6 §227; *Ag. Ap.* 2.8 §§103–4; 4Q266 6 2:2–4), apparently quarantined (*Ant.* 3.11.3 §261; 11Q19 48:16), and probably denied from reading Hebrew texts on Sabbath in a synagogue.[27] Whomever and whatever she touches would become temporarily impure. According to Marla J. Selvidge, the evangelist may have preserved the pericope of the healing of the woman with the flow of blood because it is in direct contrast to the androcentric and restrictive Levitical view which excluded a זָבָה (*zābāh*) from cultic and social life.[28]

The woman wants to be healed more than anything else in the world. She consults many physicians, probably undergoes experimental treatments, and depletes all her financial resources. Yet, she ironically derives no benefit; and her condition gradually grows worse. Her physicians must have prescribed to her numerous ancient folk remedies, such as some of those eleven treatments mentioned in the Babylonian Talmud, like drinking cumin, saffron, and fenugreek boiled in wine, placing fine flour on the bottom half of her body, and holding a barley grain found in white mule's dung for three days (*b. Šabb.* 110ab).[29] No wonder none of these remedies benefited her. She is now economically a destitute *femme seule* who endures the double burden of inadequate medical treatments and poverty. In Mark 5:26, the evangelist connotes that the inefficient medical treatments of the many ineffective physicians of the time appear to exacerbate the women's gynecological problem. It is of interest to observe that Matthew omits the entirety of Mark 5:26. Luke, on the other hand, softens Mark's scathing criticism of physicians' failure and drops out the reference to the deterioration of the physical condition of the woman. The noun ἰατρός (*iatros*, "physician"[30]), in fact, appears only twice in Mark's Gospel (2:17 [singular]; 5:26 [plural]). It seems that Mark's negative portrayal of physicians is expressed somehow differently in the Mishnah, where Rabbi Judah is quoted as saying, "The best of doctors is to Gehenna" (*m. Qidd.* 4:14).

26. On the topic of menstruation as a source of impurity and the prohibition against intercourse with a menstruant, see further Maccoby, *Ritual and Morality*, 30–46.

27. See Witherington, *Women and the Genesis of Christianity*, 3–9, who seems to suggest there are no known examples of women reading the Scriptures in the synagogues during Jesus' time, on account of the purity laws in Leviticus 15.

28. See Selvidge, "Mark 5:25–34," 623.

29. See also Lane, *Gospel According to Mark*, 192.

30. See BDAG, 465–66.

## Action and Immediacy of Healing (Mark 5:27–29)

The Markan phrase, ἀκούσασα περὶ τοῦ Ἰησοῦ (*akousasa peri tou Iēsou*, "having heard concerning Jesus," Mark 5:27), denotes that the woman with the flow of blood has certainly heard firsthand reports of Jesus' charismatic healing activity in Galilee, where the sick touch, or are touched by, Jesus to receive healing (Mark 1:31, 41; 3:10; see also 6:56; 7:33; 8:22; 10:13). Upon hearing the news of Jesus' presence, a flicker of hope rekindles her spirit, since her subjective experience with many physicians has taught her that human aid is indeed no longer a possibility. She is now prepared to place all her trust in the person of Jesus. She is strongly motivated to take the initiative and surreptitiously seek out her own healing by sneaking up behind him in the crowd and intentionally touching his outer ἱμάτιον (*himation*, "garment," "cloak," "robe," Mark 5:27[31]). One may wonder: Why does she behave with Jesus in such an unusual manner? Feeling embarrassed and ashamed of her condition and the ceremonial stigma associated with her disease? At any rate, the woman's act of touching Jesus' garment dominates the scene. This judgment is confirmed and heightened by the fact that the main verb ἅπτειν (*haptein*, "to touch," "to take hold of," "to hold," Mark 5:27[32]) appears for the first time after the employment of a series of seven descriptive participles in Mark 5:25–27 (οὖσα [*ousa*, "being"], παθοῦσα [*pathousa*, "having suffered"], δαπανήσασα [*dapanēsasa*, "having spent"], ὠφεληθεῖσα [*ōphelētheisa*, "having benefited"], ἐλθοῦσα [*elthousa*, "having become"], ἀκούσασα [*akousasa*, "having heard"], and ἐλθοῦσα [*elthousa*, "having come up"]).[33] Furthermore, approaching Jesus from behind to touch his garment requires the woman with the flow of blood to have a great deal of audacity and resolution to break through the male crowd accompanying him. Nevertheless, her touch of Jesus' garment breaks social taboos, constitutes a cultural *faux pas*, and transgresses gender boundaries. Clothes, then and now, constitute a second skin and function as a visible boundary marker between self and other. Moreover, her touch would ritually render Jesus unclean according to Jewish purity laws as prescribed in the book of Leviticus.

At this point the evangelist halts the flow of the narrative by stepping on the stage to directly supply the audience with useful and germane

---

31. See *BDAG*, 475.

32. See *BDAG*, 126.

33. See Taylor, *Gospel According to St. Mark*, 46; Marcus, *Mark 1–8*, 367; Donahue and Harrington, *Gospel of Mark*, 174; Moloney, *Gospel of Mark*, 109.

information regarding the exact motivation behind the woman's bold behavior and intention of touching Jesus' garment in public: ἔλεγεν γὰρ ὅτι Ἐὰν ἅψωμαι κἂν τῶν ἱματίων αὐτοῦ σωθήσομαι (*elegen gar hoti Ean hapsōmai kan tōn himatiōn autou sōthēsomai*, "for she was saying, 'If I even touch his garments, I shall be saved,'" Mark 5:28). Note that this concise explanatory remark, functioning as a narrative aside pointing back to Mark 5:27, is introduced by a postpositive γὰρ-clause (*gar*, "for"), a construction the evangelist is quite fond of using (e.g., Mark 1:16; 3:21; 5:42; 6:52; 9:6; 10:22; 11:13; 16:4).[34] The soliloquy of the woman with the flow of blood definitely points to her confidence and trust that her afflicted body will be restored to health if she only manages to touch Jesus' garment. There is no doubt that she regards him as a miracle-worker, whose garment, which is a spatial extension of his body, has the power to bring about a healing (see also Mark 6:56; Acts 5:15; 19:12). The notion of transmitting healing energy through touch has roots in the Hebrew Bible (1 Kgs 17:17–24; 2 Kgs 4:25–37; 13:20–21).

It is interesting to point out that Mark employs three verbs to describe Jesus' healing activity: θεραπεύειν (*therapeuein*, "to heal," Mark 1:34; 3:2, 10; 6:5, 13[35]), ἰᾶσθαι (*iasthai*, "to cure," Mark 5:29[36]), and σῴζειν (*sōzein*, "to save from death," "to save/free from disease," Mark 3:4; 5:23, 28, 34; 6:56; 10:52[37]). While the first two verbs are generally used in reference to the restitution of someone's physical health from a disease, the last verb has acquired a broad range of theological connotations, including spiritual salvation, as well as physical restoration of health. In narrating the soliloquy of the woman with the flow of blood, the evangelist uses σῴζειν (*sōzein*) to accentuate her desire to have her whole life fully made well and saved from her bodily ailment. This same verb may have played a major role in having the two pericopae of Jairus's little daughter and the woman with the flow of blood intercalated (Mark 5:23, 28).

As a result of her touch, the woman with the flow of blood experiences immediate healing from her twelve-year chronic and gynecological disease: καὶ εὐθὺς ἐξηράνθη ἡ πηγὴ τοῦ αἵματος αὐτῆς (*kai euthus exēranthē hē pēgē tou haimatos autēs*, "and immediately the fountain of her blood was dried up," Mark 5:29a). Her daring initiative of touching Jesus' garment draws

34. See further Fowler, *Let the Reader Understand*, 92–98.
35. See *BDAG*, 453.
36. See *BDAG*, 465.
37. See *BDAG*, 982–83.

out from Jesus the healing power she has desired and wanted so desperately for a long time. The phrase καὶ εὐθὺς (*kai euthus*, "and immediately," Mark 5:29a) is certainly a characteristic and idiosyncratic stylistic feature of Mark's Gospel, employed by the evangelist some twenty-five times (e.g., Mark 1:10; 2:8; 4:5; 6:45; 7:35; 8:10; 9:15; 10:52; 14:72; 15:1). It is used here to juxtapose between the twelve-year failure of many physicians in treating the woman with the flow of blood and the immediacy of healing brought forth by her bold act of touching Jesus' garment in an open space on the road close to the Sea of Galilee. The only thing the woman with the flow of blood is sure of, based on her internal experience and state, is her knowledge of the cessation of the flow of blood: καὶ ἔγνω τῷ σώματι ὅτι ἴαται ἀπὸ τῆς μάστιγος (*kai egnō tō sōmati hoti iatai apo tēs mastigos*, "and she knew in the body that she was cured from the affliction," Mark 5:29). The evangelist describes her blood-related disease as μάστιξ (*mastix*, "whip," "lash," "scourge," Mark 5:29, 34; see also 3:10[38]).

## *Dialogue between Jesus and Disciples (Mark 5:30–32)*

Jesus' immediate knowledge of the emission of healing power from his body, καὶ εὐθὺς ὁ Ἰησοῦς ἐπιγνοὺς ἐν ἑαυτῷ (*kai euthus ho Iēsous epignous en heautō*, "and immediately Jesus perceiving in himself," Mark 5:30), correlates with the woman's immediate knowledge of the healing of her body ("and she knew in the body," Mark 5:29). Both happen synchronously and inwardly. The reference to "perceiving in himself" in Mark 5:30 especially recalls Mark 2:8, where Jesus immediately perceives τῷ πνεύματι αὐτοῦ (*tō pneumati autou*, "in his spirit") the unspoken thoughts of his opponents in a house in Capernaum. In Mark's Gospel, Jesus is the unique bearer of God's Holy Spirit and the locus of God's presence on earth (Mark 1:8, 10–12, 24; 3:11; 5:7; 9:7; 15:39). Therefore, δύναμις (*dynamis*, "power," "might," Mark 5:30[39]) emitting from him is indisputably the power of God's Spirit dwelling in him. "The Spirit moves outwards from Jesus," writes Susan Miller, "casting out her disease, and she realizes through a physical change that she has been healed."[40] Put differently, Jesus' power has overridden the defiling physical condition of the woman and, consequently, healed her. This power is associated with the coming of God's reign (Mark 1:15).

38. See *BDAG*, 620–21.
39. See *BDAG*, 262–63.
40. Miller, *Women in Mark's Gospel*, 58.

The journey to Jairus's house comes to an abrupt halt as Jesus physically turns to face the crowd and asks, Τίς μου ἥψατο τῶν ἱματίων (*Tis mou hēpsato tōn himatiōn*, "Who touched my garments?," Mark 5:30). He knows that this is not an accidental touch since curative power has come out of him and healed the woman on the spot. He, moreover, knows that this touch is an expression of faith. At any rate, his question demands an answer. He will not leave until he gets an explanation. The account now shifts from narration to dialogue between Jesus and his disciples, which is a constituent part of the pericope. The disciples collectively answer Jesus' question with a counterquestion, Βλέπεις τὸν ὄχλον συνθλίβοντά σε καὶ λέγεις, Τίς μου ἥψατο (*Blepeis ton ochlon synthlibonta se kai legeis, Tis mou hēpsato*, "You see the crowd pressing upon you, and you say, 'Who touched me?,'" Mark 5:31). They seem to find his question absurd since the crowd has been jostling him all along (Mark 5:21, 24). Their incredulous reaction signifies their failure to understand him, not realizing that, through intentional physical contact, power emanates from him. Adele Y. Collins writes that the disciples' counterquestion to Jesus shows that they "have less understanding about the workings of Jesus' healing power than the woman does."[41]

Jesus ignores his disciples' response and keeps penetratingly looking around to find τὴν τοῦτο ποιήσασαν (*tēn touto poiēsasan*, "the [woman] having done this," Mark 5:32), viz., touching his outer garment. Scholars debate whether this clause reflects the knowledge of Jesus or the evangelist Mark. On the one hand, some scholars, such as Joel Marcus and Robert H. Stein, assert that it comes from the viewpoint of Jesus, whose supernatural knowledge perceives the gender of the person who touched him (cf. Mark 2:8; 8:17).[42] On the other hand, other scholars, such as William L. Lane and Adele Y. Collins, argue that it comes from Mark's perspective, and thus does not imply that Jesus knew the gender of the person who touched him.[43] Robert H. Gundry seeks to find some sort of middle-ground position. He writes that both Mark and Jesus know the sex of the person who has touched Jesus.[44] However, Jesus knows that the woman is somehow there among the crowd. His look invites her to come out from the shadow of anonymity.

41. Collins, *Mark*, 283.

42. See Marcus, *Mark 1–8*, 359; Stein, *Mark*, 270.

43. See Lane, *Gospel According to Mark*, 193; Collins, *Mark*, 283.

44. See Gundry, *Mark*, 1:271.

## Post-Healing Encounter (Mark 5:33–34)

The now-healed woman finally emerges from the shadow of her hideout and begins walking toward Jesus. Their face-to-face encounter leads to another short dialogue. She approaches him experiencing fear and trembling (Mark 5:33), which are proper human responses to the divine power working through Jesus. Like the leper man (Mark 1:40), the Gerasene demoniac (Mark 5:6), Jairus (Mark 5:22), and the Syrophoenician woman (Mark 7:25), she reverentially falls down before him and courageously tells him πᾶσαν τὴν ἀλήθειαν (pasan tēn alētheian, "the whole truth," Mark 5:33) in front of the entire crowd. The fullness of truth encompasses mentioning to Jesus her long affliction, stealthy touch of his garment, and her immediate healing (Mark 5:25–29). She really has no idea what kind of reaction to expect from him. Perhaps she thinks he will castigate her for transgressing Levitical ritual laws of purity and breaching the boundaries of cultural decency.

Far from excoriating and reprimanding the woman for not being secluded or cloistered from society, Jesus tenderly and respectfully bestows dignity on her by addressing her as Θυγάτηρ (Thygatēr, "Daughter," Mark 5:34), making her the only woman in the Gospels to be called daughter by him. Furthermore, calling her "daughter" "is a typical respectful and affectionate mode of address to females," writes Joel Marcus, "regardless of age or family relationship."[45] Jesus then confirms that, by virtue of her audacity, she has been saved: ἡ πίστις σου σέσωκέν σε (hē pistis sou sesōken se, "your faith has saved you," Mark 5:34). His words heartily commend her faith and indicate that her healing is holistic, whereby every dimension of her being—physical, emotional, mental, social, sexual, and spiritual—is restored and redeemed. The woman's trusting faith has already saved her and made her well once she touched Jesus' garment (Mark 5:27). The verb σῴζειν (sōzein) is consciously used in the perfect tense (σέσωκέν σε, sesōken se, "has saved you," Mark 5:34), denoting an action already completed, whose results continue into the present.[46] Faith, which in this context denotes trust and confidence in Jesus' curative ability, has an intrinsic power to bring about healing. In the Synoptic Gospels, faith, whether explicitly or implicitly, often relates to healing (e.g., Mark 2:5; 5:36; 6:5–6; 10:52; Matt 8:13; 15:28; Luke 17:19). Emphasizing the relationship between faith and

---

45. See Marcus, Mark 1–8, 360.
46. See Guelich, Mark 1—8:26, 299.

healing, William L. Lane correctly states, "It was *the grasp of her faith* rather than her hand that had secured the healing she sought."[47]

Jesus' twofold command brings the pericope to its completion. He commands the now-healed woman to ὕπαγε εἰς εἰρήνην (*hypage eis eirēnēn*, "go into peace/go in peace," Mark 5:34). This traditional biblical formula (Exod 4:18; Judg 18:6; 1 Sam 1:17; 20:42; 2 Sam 15:90; 2 Kgs 5:19; Tob 10:12; Jdt 8:35) indicates more than a mere human dismissal order. It is a blessing conveying a divine peace (שָׁלוֹם, *šālôm*[48]) and denoting a holistic and harmonious well-being. The peace with which Jesus dismisses the woman is permanent since she has been restored to a condition of wholeness, soundness, and "proper relationship with God."[49] Jesus' final words, καὶ ἴσθι ὑγιὴς ἀπὸ τῆς μάστιγός σου (*kai isthi hygiēs apo tēs mastigos sou*, "and be healthy from your affliction," Mark 5:34), give the woman assurance that her healing and recovery are irreversible. The now-healed woman is fully able to reclaim her body, fertility, and sexuality since her feminine identity has been profoundly saved and healed by the true physician.[50]

The pericope of Jairus's little daughter that left off in Mark 5:24 ("And he [Jesus] went with him [Jairus], and a great crowd was accompanying him [Jesus] and pressing in on him") due to the interruption caused by the pericope of the healing of the woman with the flow of blood (Mark 5:25–34), is now resumed in Mark 5:35.

---

47. Lane, *Gospel According to Mark*, 193 (italics original).

48. See *BDB*, 1022–23.

49. Schweizer, *Good News According to Mark*, 118; see also Guelich, *Mark 1—8:26*, 299–300; Stein, *Mark*, 271.

50. See further Calduch-Benages, *Perfume of the Gospel*, 16–30.

# 2

# "What Do You Desire I Should Do For You?"

## Text

46 They came to Jericho. As he and his disciples and a large crowd were leaving Jericho, Bartimaeus son of Timaeus, a blind beggar, was sitting by the roadside. 47 When he heard that it was Jesus of Nazareth, he began to shout out and say, "Jesus, Son of David, have mercy on me!" 48 Many sternly ordered him to be quiet, but he cried out even more loudly, "Son of David, have mercy on me!" 49 Jesus stood still and said, "Call him here." And they called the blind man, saying to him, "Take heart; get up, he is calling you." 50 So throwing off his cloak, he sprang up and came to Jesus. 51 Then Jesus said to him, "What do you want me to do for you?" The blind man said to him, "My teacher, let me see again." 52 Jesus said to him, "Go; your faith has made you well." Immediately he regained his sight and followed him on the way.

Mark 10:46–52 (NRSV)[1]
(See also Matt 20:29–34; Luke 18:35–43)

## Scholarly Context

THE PERICOPE OF THE blind man Bartimaeus, healed outside Jericho (Mark 10:46–52), is the last healing-miracle story in Mark's Gospel. It belongs to the Triple Tradition (Mark 10:46–52 || Matt 20:29–34 [Matt 9:27–31 is a doublet] || Luke 18:35–43). There exists a considerable consensus among scholars that the evangelist has skillfully used it to look back and form an *inclusio* with the pericope of the healing of an anonymous blind man at Bethsaida (Mark 8:22–26). These two pericopae are the only healing-miracle stories dealing with restoration of sight in the entirety of Mark's

---

1. The pericope of Mark 10:46–52 is liturgically read on the thirtieth Sunday of Ordinary Time, Cycle B.

Gospel. Noticeably, they frame the central section of the Gospel (Mark 8:22-26 [8:27—10:45] 10:46-52), which is thematically the most important, coherent, and carefully constructed block, containing a significant amount of material intended to illuminate the intrinsic correlation between Christology, soteriology, discipleship, and followership.[2]

Given that this framing is the most widely recognized example of a literary bracketing technique in Mark's Gospel,[3] one is quite justified in inferring that the evangelist has placed the pericope of the healing of the blind man Bartimaeus in its present position to heighten the symbolic and theological significance of its pivotal narrative. The traditional association of the pericope with the city of Jericho makes it, as Vernon. K. Robbins demonstrates,[4] function as a perfect binding and transitional link between the previous three chapters dealing with Jesus being *en route* to Jerusalem (Mark 8:27—10:45) and the next three chapters focusing on Jesus being in and around Jerusalem (Mark 11:1—13:37), which ultimately culminates in his passion, death, and resurrection (Mark 14:1—16:8).

It has been customary with most scholars to mention the significance of the deep ironic symbolism embedded in the pericope of the healing of the blind man Bartimaeus, which certainly sheds new interpretive light on the themes of faith, discipleship, and followership.[5] Within the larger context of the central section of Mark's Gospel (Mark 8:22-26 [8:27—10:45] 10:46-52), Bartimaeus's faith stands in sharp contrast to the disciples' lack of faith. Throughout this section, the disciples are imperceptive to the fact that Jesus, whom Peter, speaking on their behalf, acclaims as ὁ Χριστός (*ho Christos*, "the Christ," Mark 8:29), is also ὁ υἱὸς τοῦ ἀνθρώπου (*ho huios tou anthrōpou*, "the son of the man," "the Son of Man"), who is destined to suffer, die, and rise. Thus, immediately after Peter's confession, Jesus progressively makes three predictions about his impending passion-death-resurrection (Mark 8:31-32a; 9:30-31; 10:32-34). After each prediction, the disciples ironically exhibit a complete lack of understanding of his imminent vicarious death (Mark 8:32b; 9:32-34; 10:35-41), which prompts

---

2. See further Perrin, *What Is Redaction Criticism?*, 43-44; Achtemeier, "'And He Followed Him,'" 132-33; Marcus, *Way of the Lord*, 32; Iersel, *Mark*, 84-85; France, *Gospel of Mark*, 320-21; Malbon, *Hearing Mark*, 56; Green, *Way of the Cross*, 35-38.

3. See Fowler, *Let the Reader Understand*, 144; Rhoads et al., *Mark as Story*, 52; Collins, *Mark*, 506; Stein, *Mark*, 491.

4. See Robbins, "Healing of Blind Bartimaeus," 236-41.

5. See Perrin, *New Testament*, 155-58; Kelber, *Mark's Story*, 44; Senior, *Passion of Jesus*, 32; Marcus, *Mark 8-16*, 588-89.

him to instruct them on the meaning and cost of authentic discipleship (Mark 8:33—9:1; 9:35–37; 10:42–45).

The disciples' imperceptiveness, as a matter of fact, renders them spiritually blind. In fact, as John E. Skinner notes, "Spiritual blindness is a much worse affliction than physical blindness."[6] The evangelist has already alluded to their lack of faith (Mark 4:40), hardness of heart (Mark 6:52), blindness and deafness (Mark 8:18), and lack of understanding (Mark 8:21). So conspicuous is the ironic symbolism of the juxtaposition of the physical blindness of Bartimaeus, who is an outsider, with the spiritual myopia of the disciples, who belong to Jesus' inner circle: the former acclaims Jesus twice as Υἱὲ Δαυὶδ (*Huie Dauid,* "Son of David," Mark 10:47–48), gets his eyesight restored, and becomes an exemplar of faith, discipleship, and followership,[7] while the latter remain spiritually obtuse, and their behavior is customarily counterproductive. Take into consideration the following scenarios. First, after hearing Jesus' comment about how welcoming children amounts to welcoming him (Mark 9:33–37), the disciples collectively rebuke people who bring children to Jesus to be touched by him either for healing or blessing purposes (Mark 10:13–16). Second, after their failure to cast out an unclean spirit from a boy (Mark 9:14–29), John and the eleven disciples directly try to stop an unknown and successful exorcist from performing exorcisms in Jesus' name just because he does not belong to Jesus' inner circle (Mark 9:38–39). Third, after listening to Jesus' remark about self-denial and cross-bearing (Mark 8:34–37), James and John make an ambitious request of Jesus to grant them worldly honor and prestige, which naturally irritates the other ten disciples (Mark 10:35–37).

Moreover, the pericope of the healing of the blind man Bartimaeus invites comparison with other stories in Mark's larger narrative context. Indeed, in many remarkable respects it resembles the pericope of the healing of the woman with the flow of blood (Mark 5:25–34). Clearly, both the woman and Bartimaeus are (1) minor characters who appear only once within the entirety of Mark's Gospel; (2) afflicted by a physical disease (Mark 5:25; 10:46); (3) marginalized and desperate (Mark 5:26–27; 10:46–48); and (4) boldly persistent in pursuing Jesus' healing power (Mark 5:27–28; 10:47–48). Along with this, one also can recognize that both pericopae have the motif of hearing (Mark 5:27; 10:47) and the motif of faith (Mark

6. Skinner, *Christian Disciple,* 68.

7. See Schweizer, *Good News According to Mark,* 116; Malbon, *In the Company of Jesus,* 200; Ossandón, "Bartimaeus' Faith," 384.

5:34; 10:52). In so many ways, the pericope of the healing of the blind man Bartimaeus also stands out in most striking contrast to the pericope of an anonymous wealthy man (Mark 10:17–22). Both Bartimaeus and the wealthy man are minor characters who encounter Jesus along the way. Jesus explicitly invites the latter to discipleship, "come follow me" (Mark 10:21). But his attachment to material possessions hinders him from being receptive to Jesus' invitation (Mark 10:22). In contrast, Bartimaeus leaves behind his only possession, viz., his outer ἱμάτιον (*himation*, "garment," "cloak," "robe," Mark 10:50), and follows Jesus (Mark 10:52). There is no doubt that, at the narrative level of Mark's Gospel, the evangelist presents Bartimaeus, in contrast to Jesus' disciples and the wealthy rich man, as the only male character who clearly sees Jesus for who he is when he subsequently, unconditionally, follows him on the way up to Jerusalem.

## Literary Genre and Structure

The literary genre of the pericope of the blind man Bartimaeus defies any neat form-critical classification.[8] There is no doubt that a healing miracle does exist within the pericope. Rudolf Bultmann himself catalogs it as a healing-miracle story. However, he casts doubt on the existence of "an original, conventionally narrated miracle"[9] as the basis of Mark 10:46–52. Robert H. Gundry conversely states that the pericope has a typical three-fold pattern characteristic of healing miracles.[10] First, the *description of disease* provides a brief exposition of the patient's illness: Bartimaeus begs alongside the Jericho road because of his blindness (Mark 10:46). Second, the *healing of disease* shows that the patient's illness is exclusively remedied and cured by the miracle worker: Jesus asks Bartimaeus what he wants done for him and, consequently, restores his sight (Mark 10:49, 51–52a). Third, the *proof of healing* shows at least some confirmation of the success of the miracle itself: Bartimaeus follows Jesus on the way (Mark 10:52b) instead of sitting by the road.

The pericope also has a cluster of at least twelve literary motifs parallel to ancient Jewish, Hellenistic, and Greco-Roman healing-miracle stories.[11] They are:

8. See Marshall, *Faith as a Theme*, 125.
9. Bultmann, *History of the Synoptic Tradition*, 213.
10. See Gundry, *Mark*, 2:596.
11. See Theissen, *Miracle Stories*, 47–72.

1. The Coming of the Miracle-Worker ("And he, going out from Jericho," Mark 10:46).

2. The Appearance of the Crowd (". . . and a large crowd," Mark 10:46; ". . . many," Mark 10:48).

3. The Appearance of the Distressed Person (". . . the son of Timaeus, Bartimaeus," Mark 10:46; ". . . [he] came," Mark 10:50).

4. Reasons Given for the Appearance of the "Opposite Numbers" (". . . and having heard that it is Jesus the Nazarene," Mark 10:47).

5. Description of the Distress (". . . blind," Mark 10:46).

6. Difficulties in the Approach (". . . and many were rebuking him so that he should be silent," Mark 10:48).

7. Cries for Help (". . . he began to cry out," Mark 10:47; ". . . but he was crying out much more," Mark 10:48).

8. Pleas and Expressions of Trust ("Son of David, Jesus, have mercy on me," Mark 10:47; "Son of David, have mercy on me," Mark 10:48; ". . . that I may see [again]," Mark 10:51).

9. Assurance ("Take heart, arise, he is calling you," Mark 10:49; ". . . your faith has saved you," Mark 10:52).

10. Recognition of the Miracle (". . . and immediately he received sight," Mark 10:52).

11. Demonstration (". . . and he was following him," Mark 10:52).

12. Dismissal ("Go," Mark 10:52).

Yet, it has been postulated that the nucleus of the present pericope is not a healing-miracle story but rather a call story.[12] Paul J. Achtemeier, for example, strongly argues that the healing of Bartimaeus may have originally functioned as the account of how he became a disciple of Jesus. He contends that the healing itself assumes secondary importance and is subordinated to the call of Bartimaeus.[13] Apparently it is further claimed that a number of elements which lie at the heart of the present pericope are typical features associated with a call story. Here are some:

---

12. See further Steinhauser, "Part of a 'Call Story'?" 204–6; Steinhauser, "Form of the Bartimaeus Narrative," 583–95.

13. See Achtemeier, *Jesus and the Miracle Tradition*, 146–51.

1. The mention of the name of Bartimaeus (Mark 10:46) is atypical, since direct recipients of Jesus' healing power are never named in Mark's Gospel.[14]

2. The threefold use of the verb φωνεῖν (*phōnein*, "to call to oneself," "to summon," "to invite," Mark 10:49[15]) is apparently synonymous with the verb καλεῖν (*kalein*; Mark 1:20; 2:17; 3:31[16]).[17]

3. The mention of throwing away the garment (Mark 10:50) represents that which a person leaves behind to follow Jesus (Mark 1:18, 20; 10:28).[18]

4. The use of the verb ἀκολουθεῖν (*akolouthein*, "to follow," Mark 10:52[19]), which is a technical term used in the sense of becoming a follower or disciple of Jesus (Mark 1:18; 2:14; 8:34; 10:21, 28; 15:41).[20]

5. The combination of ἀκολουθεῖν (*akolouthein*, "to follow," Mark 10:52) with the Markan theological term ἐν τῇ ὁδῷ (*en tē hodō*, "on the way," Mark 10:52) is a strong indication of Markan description of Christian followership or discipleship.

It is of course possible that the pericope of the blind man Bartimaeus is a mixture of two literary genres.[21] In order to better appreciate the entire pericope as it stands, it is necessary that both miraculous and calling elements go hand in hand. "Any attempt to consider the passage," writes Joel Williams, "simply as a miracle story or as a call story would inevitably result in certain parts being ignored."[22]

In terms of literary structure, the pericope develops in four scenes: (1) introduction and description (Mark 10:46), (2) importunate twofold cry out for mercy (Mark 10:47–48), (3) confrontation and response (Mark 10:49–50), and (4) action and immediacy of healing (Mark 10:51–52).

---

14. See Dibelius, *From Tradition to Gospel*, 51–53; Bultmann, *History of the Synoptic Tradition*, 213.

15. See *BDAG*, 1071.

16. See *BDAG*, 502–4.

17. See Menken, "Call of Blind Bartimaeus," 277.

18. See Culpepper, "Mark 10:50," 131–32.

19. See *BDAG*, 36.

20. See Collins, *Mark*, 510; Marcus, *Mark 8–16*, 761; Stein, *Mark*, 497.

21. See Stein, *Mark*, 491; Focant, *Gospel According to Mark*, 440.

22. Williams, *Other Followers*, 169.

## Narrative Analysis

### Introduction and Description (Mark 10:46)

For the first time in Mark's Gospel, Jesus and his entourage, viz., his disciples and the accompanying crowd (Mark 10:32), make a stop at Jericho *en route* to Jerusalem. Jericho is believed to be the world's lowest city, lying about more than 800 feet below sea level, and the world's oldest continuously inhabited city, dating back to 8,000 BCE. It is about four miles from the Jordan River to the west. One needs to distinguish between two archaeological sites pertaining to the city of Jericho. The new Hasmonean/Herodian Jericho of the New Testament (Mark 10:46; Luke 19:1), identified with Tulul Abu al-ʿAlayiq, is about a mile southwest from the ancient Canaanite/Israelite Jericho of the Hebrew Bible (Num 22:1; 26:3; Josh 2; 6; 2 Sam 10:5; 2 Kgs 2:5; Ezra 2:34), identified with Tell es-Sultan. Both are now located in the Palestinian region of West Bank.[23]

Most scholars hold that the opening verse, Καὶ ἔρχονται εἰς Ἰεριχώ (*Kai erchontai eis Ierichō*, "And they come into Jericho," Mark 10:46a), betrays Markan redactional activity,[24] since the evangelist frequently employs the historic present tense verb of ἔρχεσθαι (*erchesthai*, "to come," "to go"[25]), followed by εἰς (*eis*, "into," "to") to introduce a location, such as a house (Mark 3:20), Jesus' hometown (Mark 6:1), Bethsaida (Mark 8:22), region of Judea and beyond the Jordan (Mark 10:1), Jerusalem (Mark 11:15), and Gethsemane (Mark 14:32). Strangely enough, the arrival at Jericho is immediately followed by a traditional clause, καὶ ἐκπορευομένου αὐτοῦ ἀπὸ Ἰεριχώ (*kai ekporeuomenou autou apo Ierichō*, "and he, going out from Jericho," Mark 10:46b), using a singular present genitive absolute participle of the verb ἐκπορεύεσθαι (*ekporeuesthai*, "to go out"[26]) to report the solitary departure of Jesus out of Jericho. Although Mark mentions Jesus' arrival at and departure from Jericho, he neither specifies a place where Jesus stays nor what he does in Jericho. Luke, however, writes that Jesus spends the

---

23. See further Kelso, "New Testament Jericho," 34–43; Holland and Netzer, "Jericho," 723–40; Murphy-O'Connor, *Holy Land*, 327–31.

24. See Dibelius, *From Tradition to Gospel*, 52; Schweizer, *Good News According to Mark*, 224; Achtemeier, *Jesus and the Miracle Tradition*, 142; Stein, *Mark*, 493; Robbins, "Healing of Blind Bartimaeus," 228; Johnson, "Mark 10:46–52," 191–92; Marcus, *Mark 8–16*, 759; Collins, *Mark*, 505.

25. See *BDAG*, 393–95.

26. See *BDAG*, 308–9.

night in the house of Zacchaeus, the chief toll collector at Jericho (Luke 19:1–10), after healing a blind man (Luke 18:35–42).

Jesus' arrival at Jericho, which is just fifteen miles northeast of Jerusalem, has geographical and theological importance in Mark's Gospel. Geographically, it marks a progression in Jesus' movement from the territory of Caesarea Philippi (Mark 8:27), north of the Sea of Galilee, to Judea and its capital city of Jerusalem (Mark 11:1) in the south—a journey of approximately 100 miles. Theologically, it brings Jesus closer to his destination, viz., Jerusalem, to fulfill his destiny as the messianic Son of Man who is unflinchingly going up to Jerusalem "to give his life a ransom for many" (Mark 10:45). Jesus' arrival at Jericho must have happened on Friday where he and his entourage had spent the Sabbath day there. Thus, the entire pericope of healing the blind man Bartimaeus (Mark 10:46–52) must have taken place on Palm Sunday morning, ahead of Jesus' entry into Jerusalem late that Sunday afternoon (Mark 11:1–11).[27]

Jesus now departs from Jericho probably on Sunday morning, accompanied by his disciples and a sizable crowd of people, making his pilgrimage toward Jerusalem to celebrate the Jewish Passover festival there on Thursday evening (Mark 14:12–26). He must have walked uphill on the road connecting Jericho to Jerusalem through the Jordan Valley and across the Judean Desert. It is well attested that this road was notoriously infested with highway thugs (cf. Luke 10:25–37).

The evangelist immediately introduces a new character, thus deliberately shifting the focus of attention from Jesus' departure from Jericho to ὁ υἱὸς Τιμαίου Βαρτιμαῖος, τυφλὸς προσαίτης, ἐκάθητο παρὰ τὴν ὁδόν (*ho huios Timaiou Bartimaios, typhlos prosaitēs, ekathēto para tēn hodon*, "the son of Timaeus, Bartimaeus, a blind beggar, was sitting beside the road," Mark 10:46c). This laconic description, which sets the stage on which this pericope will unfold, provides three important facts about the name, disease, and occupation of this minor character. First, it is clear that ὁ υἱὸς Τιμαίου (*ho huios Timaiou*, "the son of Timaeus," Mark 10:46c) is a translation of Bartimaeus's patronymic and hybrid name. Etymologically speaking, Βαρτιμαῖος (*Bartimaios*, "Bartimaeus," Mark 10:46c[28]) is a combination of the Aramaic prefix בַּר (*bār*, "son of"[29]) and the noun Τιμαῖος (*Timaios*; cf. *Ag. Ap.* 1.3 §16), which could be derived either from an Aramaic root verb

---

27. See Gundry, *Mark*, 2:606.
28. See *BDAG*, 167.
29. See *BDAG*, 1085.

טָמֵא (*ṭāmē᾽*, "unclean," "filthy"[30]) or from a Greek root word τιμαῖος (*timaios*, "highly prized," "valuable," "honored").[31] Since the evangelist is writing in Greek to a Greek-speaking audience, it is to be expected that he, as Joel Marcus states, "underlines the Greek connotation of the name."[32]

In Mark's Gospel, Aramaic and Hebrew words are normally listed first, followed immediately by either ὅ ἐστιν (*ho estin*, "which is," Mark 3:17; 5:41; 7:11, 34; 15:42) or ὅ ἐστιν μεθερμηνευόμενον (*ho estin methermēneuomenon*, "which, translated, is," Mark 5:41; 15:22, 34), and then translated into Greek (Mark 12:42; 15:16). Mark 10:46c lacks ὅ ἐστιν [μεθερμηνευόμενον], and the word order is anomalously reversed: the Greek translation, ὁ υἱὸς Τιμαίου (*ho huios Timaiou*, "the son of Timaeus"), precedes the Aramaic name of Βαρτιμαῖος (*Bartimaios*, "Bartimaeus"). This may reflect a pre-Markan tradition. However, Robert H. Stein proposes that the evangelist may have changed the word order to balance the word order of Bartimaeus's acclamation "Son of David, Jesus" in Mark 10:47.[33]

It is worth mentioning that Bartimaeus is the only direct recipient of Jesus' healing activity whose name is given in the entirety of Mark's Gospel. Richard Bauckham persuasively argues that the Gospels have preserved proper names of minor characters, such as Jairus (Mark 5:22), Bartimaeus (Mark 10:46), Zacchaeus (Luke 19:2), and Cleopas (Luke 24:18), "presumably because they were well-known in the early Christian movement."[34] Martin Dibelius supposes that the mention of the name Bartimaeus is an indication that the blind beggar "became a follower of Jesus, and, later, a member of the Church."[35] Interestingly enough, the evangelists Matthew and Luke, who have reproduced the Markan pericope of healing of the blind man Bartimaeus, though with different focuses, omit the phrase "the son of Timaeus, Bartimaeus" from their pericopae (Matt 20:29-34; Luke 18:35-43), presumably because he was no longer known to them or to their communities.

---

30. See *BDB*, 379-80.

31. See Taylor, *Gospel According to St. Mark*, 447-48; Gundry, *Mark*, 2:599; Collins, *Mark*, 508-9.

32. Marcus, *Mark 8-16*, 759; see also Donahue and Harrington, *Gospel of Mark*, 317; Stein, *Mark*, 494.

33. See Stein, *Mark*, 494.

34. Bauckham, *Jesus and the Eyewitnesses*, 53.

35. Dibelius, *From Tradition to Gospel*, 53.

Second, Bartimaeus suffers from ophthalmic disease. The evangelist does not state whether his blindness is congenital or adventitious. Blindness was common in antiquity. It was probably one of the most feared debilitating diseases because of its propensity to dehumanize and ostracize the blind person by reducing him or her to a socioeconomic situation of extreme helplessness, hopelessness, and dependency.[36] It was perceived and interpreted, whether temporary or permanent, as divine punishment for sin and wrongdoing (Gen 19:11; Deut 28:28; Zech 12:4; John 9:2; Acts 9:8–9; 13:11). It was also considered incurable by physicians, and only God and the Messiah can restore sight to the blind (Isa 29:18; 35:5; 42:7; Ps 146:8; 4Q504 2:14–15; 4Q521 2:7). It is not a coincidence, then, that Peter's acclamation of Jesus as "the Messiah" (Mark 8:29) takes place after the two-stage healing miracle of an anonymous blind man at Bethsaida (Mark 8:22–26).

Third, Bartimaeus, whose name probably means "son of honorable," is ironically now a beggar sitting just outside Jericho along the edge of the road to Jerusalem. Begging is considered shameful (cf. Luke 16:3), and a worse calamity that befalls a human being than poverty. A life reduced to begging appalls, for example, Ben Sira, a second-century BCE Jewish saga, who writes, "My child, do not lead the life of a beggar; it is better to die than to beg" (Sir 40:28 NRSV). It is clear that, for Ben Sira, begging constitutes a social death sentence.[37] As a blind man, Bartimaeus's only means of livelihood depends on soliciting alms. However, he is wise enough to choose a perfect spot to station himself on the road leading out of Jericho up to Jerusalem, and in doing so, makes himself visible to the heavy traffic of Passover pilgrims who must pass by him. This would, as Robert H. Gundry mentions, "provide him with an excellent opportunity to beg alms successfully."[38]

### Importunate Twofold Cry Out for Mercy (Mark 10:47–48)

The motif of hearing (ἀκούειν, akouein, "to hear," "to listen"[39]) plays an important role in Mark's Gospel. Immediately upon hearing of Jesus'

36. An exception would be the Alexandrian theologian Didymus the Blind (ca. 313–398 CE), who, despite losing his eyesight at the age of four, became a figure of immense renown, and might have headed the Alexandrian catechetical school.

37. See Wright and Camp, "Who Has Been Tested?," 79–80.

38. Gundry, Mark, 2:600.

39. See BDAG, 37–38.

presence, people who are in distress, such as the four litter-bearers of the paralytic (Mark 2:1–3), the crowd (Mark 3:7–8; 6:55), the woman with the flow of blood (Mark 5:27), and the Syrophoenician woman (Mark 7:25), are brazenly prompted to seek Jesus' miraculous healing power. Bartimaeus is no exception. Thus, καὶ ἀκούσας ὅτι Ἰησοῦς ὁ Ναζαρηνός ἐστιν (*kai ak-ousas hoti Iēsous ho Nazarēnos estin*, "and having heard that it is Jesus the Nazarene," Mark 10:47), indicates that Bartimaeus must have already heard firsthand reports regarding Jesus' ability and fame as a charismatic miracle-worker. The Markan term, "Jesus the Nazarene," is simply a reference to Nazareth as Jesus' hometown (Mark 1:24; 14:67; 16:6). A dawn of hope appears on the horizon. Bartimaeus understands that he must seize this moment of Jesus passing by. From his stationary begging spot, he raucously begins to cry out from the depths of his heart, hoping to attract Jesus' attention, Υἱὲ Δαυὶδ Ἰησοῦ, ἐλέησόν με (*Huie Dauid Iēsou, eleēson me*, "Son of David, Jesus, have mercy on me," Mark 10:47). Bartimaeus's appeal for mercy definitely echoes the cry of the afflicted to God, חָנֵּנִי יְהוָה (*ḥānnēnî Yěhwâh*, "be gracious to me, Yahweh"[40]), found in the MT of the Psalter (e.g., Pss 6:3; 9:14; 25:16; 31:10; 41:5; 57:2; 86:3; 123:3). But what about Bartimaeus's designation of Jesus as "Son of David?"

David was the second monarch of the unified monarchy of Judah-Israel (ruled ca. 1000–960 BCE), who conquered Jerusalem and made it the capital city of the unified monarchy (2 Sam 5:1–7). It is generally believed, among the various messianic expectations of the Hebrew Bible, the Pseudepigrapha, the Qumran, and the New Testament writings, that the Messiah, the future king who would rule over Israel and inaugurate God's peaceful reign in the world, would be a descendant of David (e.g., 2 Sam 7:8–16; Pss 2:7; 89:3–4, 20–39; 110:1; 132:1–12; Isa 11:1–5; Jer 23:5–6; Mic 5:2–5; Zech 9:9–10; Pss. Sol. 17:21; 2 Esd 12:31–32; 4Q252 6; Matt 1:1; Luke 1:32; John 7:41–42; Acts 2:25–31; Rom 1:3; 2 Tim 2:8; Heb 7:14; Rev 5:5). Thus, Bartimaeus's acclamation of Jesus as "Son of David," which is a designation appearing twice for the first time in Mark's Gospel in this pericope (Mark 10:47–48), likely points to his understanding of Jesus' identity as a Davidic messianic figure.[41] "What Bartimaeus lacks in eyesight," writes James R. Edwards, "he makes up for in insight."[42] Ironically, he intuitively

---

40. See *BDB*, 335–36.

41. See Lane, *Gospel According to Mark*, 387–88; Collins, *Mark*, 509–10; Stein, *Mark*, 494–95.

42. Edwards, *Gospel According to Mark*, 329.

sees who Jesus is more clearly than those with perfect sight, including the disciples who have been with him all along. If it can be granted that Mark's Gospel was addressed to the gentile Christian community in Rome, at least provisionally, then Bartimaeus's association of Jesus with David would undoubtedly make sense to Mark's audience (cf. Rom 1:3).

The designation, "Son of David," was associated in first-century CE Judaism with King Solomon (e.g., 4Q398 11–13), David's son with Bathsheba (2 Sam 12:24), who is depicted as a miracle-healer and an exorcist *par excellence* (e.g., Wis 7:15–21; T. Sol. 18; 20:1; 11QapPsa; L.A.B. 60:3; *Ant.* 8.2.5 §§42–46). This has led a significant number of scholars to conclude that Bartimaeus's acclamation should be understood against this Solomonic background.[43] Consequently, James H. Charlesworth concludes that "the most probable explanation of Bartimaeus' υἱὸς Δαυίδ is some Solomonic denotation."[44] According to this interpretation, Bartimaeus, in a nutshell, identifies Jesus as a healer, like Solomon, who brings salvation. Robert H. Gundry convincingly argues that Bartimaeus's acclamation scarcely calls Solomon to mind; but rather it points to Yahweh's servant, a descendent of David, whose ministry includes the healing of blindness (LXX Isa 29:18; 35:5–6; 61:1; Ezek 34:23–24).[45] He contends that "perhaps the actuality of Jesus' ministry and reputation as a healer leads via these OT passages to his being called 'Son of David' in a plea for the mercy of a healing."[46] Moreover, Richard Bauckham also disagrees with the scholarly Solomonic interpretation because the designation "Son of David" is important to Mark's composition and "serves to introduce the theme of Jesus' kingship that runs through his passion narrative from the triumphal entry (cf. 11:10) onwards (cf. 12:35–37; 14:61–62; 15:2, 9, 12, 18, 26, 32)."[47]

Many unidentified people in the crowd, probably including Jesus' disciples, are disgusted and agitated by Bartimaeus's exasperating behavior. They aggressively ἐπετίμων αὐτῷ (*epetimon auto*, "were rebuking him," Mark 10:48) to remain silent. This is the last time the verb ἐπιτιμᾶν

---

43. See further Meier, *Marginal Jew*, 2:688–89; Donahue and Harrington, *Gospel of Mark*, 319; Moloney, *Gospel of Mark*, 208–9; Marcus, *Mark 8–16*, 762–63.

44. Charlesworth, "Son of David," 87.

45. See Gundry, *Mark*, 2:600–1.

46. Gundry, *Mark*, 2:601.

47. Bauckham, *Jesus and the Eyewitnesses*, 599; see also Focant, *Gospel According to Mark*, 440–41.

(*epitiman*, "to rebuke," "to censure," "to warn sternly"[48]) appears in Mark's Gospel. It is generally employed by Jesus to scold demonic (Mark 1:25; 3:12; 9:25), cosmic (Mark 4:39), and human negative forces (Mark 8:30, 33). It is also used by Peter, who rebukes Jesus (Mark 8:32), and the disciples, who rebuke people bringing children to Jesus to place his hands on them (Mark 10:13). Mark does not explain the reason behind the animosity and contemptuousness of the unidentified people toward Bartimaeus. They might have thought that he wanted to capitalize on this opportunity. Or perhaps, they did not want anyone, especially someone who was a nobody, to trouble Jesus, who was *en route* to Jerusalem. Interestingly, what is happening right now is a visible clash of voices between the plea of Bartimaeus for mercy and the attempt of the unidentified people to silence him. Bartimaeus refuses to bow down to their negative verbal and emotional repertoire, as well as their rigid social propriety. Undeterred, he cries out even louder, "Son of David, have mercy on me!" (Mark 10:48). Note that Bartimaeus's second cry out for mercy lacks any reference to the proper name of Jesus.

## Confrontation and Response (Mark 10:49–50)

Bartimaeus's persistence wins out. Jesus stands still (στάς, *stas*, "having stood," Mark 10:49). The pilgrimage to Jerusalem is interrupted and comes to an abrupt stop. Jesus has heard Bartimaeus's twofold cry out for mercy. Thus, he takes the initiative in confronting those whose rebuke has futilely attempted to silence Bartimaeus by commanding them to call the blind man to come to him. Jesus' command, Φωνήσατε αὐτόν (*phōnēsate auton*, "Call him," Mark 10:49), definitely brings about a change in their negative attitudes toward Bartimaeus. They sheepishly tell him now words of encouragement, saying: Θάρσει, ἔγειρε, φωνεῖ σε (*Tharsei, egeire, phōnei se*, "take heart, arise, he is calling you," Mark 10:49). The verbs θαρσεῖν (*tharsein*, "be enheartened," "be courageous"[49]) and ἐγείρειν (*egeirein*, "to get up"[50]) are used in the imperative. The first one denotes comfort, while the second requires motion. An invitation has been extended. All the invitee, viz., Bartimaeus, has to do right now is make his way toward the inviter, viz., Jesus, no matter the difficulties.

48. See *BDAG*, 384.

49. See *BDAG*, 444.

50. See *BDAG*, 271–72.

Bartimaeus responds to the invitation with obedience and alacrity. Mark vividly captures his euphoria and enthusiasm in one sentence: ἀποβαλὼν τὸ ἱμάτιον αὐτοῦ ἀναπηδήσας ἦλθεν πρὸς τὸν Ἰησοῦν (*apobalōn to himation autou anapēdēsas ēlthen pros ton Iēsoun*, "casting aside his garment, having jumped up, he came to Jesus," Mark 10:50). Bartimaeus throws away his outer garment, which is the most important piece of property he owns (Exod 22:26–27). His gesture is symbolically and dramatically powerful. He no longer puts his trust in the outer garment he has used for a long time to spread out on the street to receive and collect alms. "The fact that he throws his cloak aside and springs up," writes Martin Dibelius, "only shows his readiness and his confidence, in short, his faith."[51] Moreover, Bartimaeus jumps up on his feet and walks away from his stationary begging spot to present himself, apparently unassisted, to Jesus. Matthew and Luke leave out the graphic verse of Mark 10:50.

### Action and Immediacy of Healing (Mark 10:51–52)

Son of David (Jesus) and Son of Timaeus (Bartimaeus) now stand facing each other. It is a moment of great anticipation and hope. Far from rebuking him for using the designation "Son of David" (Mark 10:47–48),[52] Jesus, without further ado, cuts right to the chase and asks the blind man the million-dollar question: Τί σοι θέλεις ποιήσω (*Ti soi theleis poiēsō*, "What do you desire I should do for you?" Mark 10:51). Jesus' question obviously intends to initiate a dialogue with Bartimaeus and thus provides him with a once-in-a-lifetime opportunity to reveal what matters most to him. It is worth mentioning that Jesus' question to Bartimaeus is identical to his question to James and John (Mark 10:36). Disappointingly enough, their response is shortsighted, expressing a desire to attain privileged and prestigious status (Mark 10:37), which in turn highlights their spiritual blindness. Bartimaeus, by contrast, desires the only thing he desperately needs, and that is an act of mercy. He tells Jesus, Ραββουνι, ἵνα ἀναβλέψω (*Rabbouni, hina anablepsō*, "Rabbouni, that I may see [again],"

51. Dibelius, *From Tradition to Gospel*, 52.

52. Jesus also does not rebuke the many unidentified people who associate his first-time entry into Jerusalem with the coming of King David's kingdom (Mark 11:1–11). However, he later calls into question the scribal (mis)understanding and teaching that the Messiah is King David's son. Quoting Psalm 110:1, he points out that King David himself identifies the Messiah as his Lord, not his son (Mark 12:35–37). For Jesus, the Messiah is more than King David's son.

Mark 10:51). Ραββουνι (*Rabbouni*) is a transliteration of the Aramaic word רַבּוּנִי (*rabbônî*, "my Lord," "my lord," "my master," "my teacher"[53]), which in turn is a heightened form of ῥαββί (*rabbi*; Hebrew: רַבִּי, *rabbî*, Mark 9:5; 11:21; 14:45). It is only used twice in the four Gospels—once by Bartimaeus and once by Mary Magdalene (John 20:16). It is a diminutive form of endearment, expressing a respectful attitude toward and a personal faith in Jesus. It is used in "rabbinic literature," says Robert H. Gundry, "in addresses to God but not in addresses to human beings."[54] Note that the evangelist does not translate into Greek the Aramaic word Ραββουνι (*Rabbouni*) for his audience.

Bartimaeus desires and hopes that Jesus can and will restore his vision. The compound verb ἀναβλέπειν (*anablepein*, "to look up," "to regain sight," Mark 10:51[55]) can be construed in two ways in English. On the one hand, it means to receive sight for the first time. If so, then Bartimaeus's blindness is congenital; and his request should be translated as "that I may see." On the other hand, the compound verb also means to regain the ability to see again. If so, then Bartimaeus's blindness is adventitious; and his plea should be translated as "that I may see again." Based on the Johannine account of a man born blind, where the compound verb is used in connection with Jesus' restoring sight to him (John 9:11, 15, 18), Joel Marcus theorizes that it is possible that Bartimaeus had been blind from birth.[56] However, Robert H. Gundry favors "the restoration of sight" due to "the omission of any indication that Bartimaeus was born blind."[57]

Jesus' words to Bartimaeus, Ὕπαγε, ἡ πίστις σου σέσωκέν σε (*Hypage, hē pistis sou sesōken se*, "Go, your faith has saved you," Mark 10:52), recall his praise to the woman with the flow of blood (Mark 5:34). Faith is an indispensable prerequisite for receiving healing. In Mark's Gospel, faith ultimately connotes trust in Jesus' therapeutic power despite all difficulties and barriers. The sheer audacity and tenacity of Bartimaeus points to his faith; he boldly hails Jesus as "Son of David," and firmly refuses attempts to silence his pleas for mercy. As a result, his sight is restored immediately (εὐθὺς, *euthus*, Mark 10:52[58]). As he opens his eyes for the first time, he

53. See *BDAG*, 902; *BDB*, 912.
54. Gundry, *Mark*, 2:602.
55. See *BDAG*, 59.
56. See Marcus, *Mark 8–16*, 761.
57. Gundry, *Mark*, 2:603; see also Loos, *Miracles of Jesus*, 425.
58. See *BDAG*, 406.

sees the face of his healer, probably smiling at him. He is now able to see that Jesus is the authentic expression of God's redemptive power and mercy. Jesus does what only the God of Israel can do (Isa 35:4–6). Unlike the two-stage healing of the anonymous blind man at Bethsaida (Mark 8:22–26), there are no ritualistic or magical elements, not even a physical touch, used in the healing process of Bartimaeus—only words. There are several accounts in the Gospels, such as those of the paralytic man (Mark 2:1–12), the man with a withered hand (Mark 3:1–6), the daughter of the Syrophoenician woman (Mark 7:24–30), the servant of the centurion (Matt 8:5–13), the ten lepers (Luke 17:11–19), and the lame man (John 5:1–9), where Jesus accomplishes healings directly and concretely by the agency of his word alone. Jesus demonstrates by his words that it is the trusting confidence of faith within Bartimaeus that has saved and healed him from his physical blindness.

Having gained the ability to see, Bartimaeus does the unthinkable. Instead of going back to his family, he disregards Jesus' dismissal command and voluntarily follows him ἐν τῇ ὁδῷ (en tē hodō, "on the way," Mark 10:52). This Markan theological phrase, which appears in the beginning (Mark 8:27), middle (Mark 9:33–34), and end (Mark 10:32) of the central section of the Gospel (Mark 8:27—10:45) certainly means, in its essence, following Jesus on the way of ultimate self-denial and cross-bearing. The evangelist presents the newly sighted Bartimaeus as a disciple who follows Jesus along the way to Jerusalem (Mark 11:1), where passion, death, and resurrection await Jesus, the Son of Man (Mark 14:62), the Son of God (Mark 15:39).

# 3

# "Shall I Come Heal Him?"

## Text

5 When he entered Capernaum, a centurion came to him, appealing to him 6 and saying, "Lord, my servant is lying at home paralyzed, in terrible distress." 7 And he said to him, "I will come and cure him." 8 The centurion answered, "Lord, I am not worthy to have you come under my roof; but only speak the word, and my servant will be healed. 9 For I also am a man under authority, with soldiers under me; and I say to one, 'Go,' and he goes, and to another, 'Come,' and he comes, and to my slave, 'Do this,' and the slave does it." 10 When Jesus heard him, he was amazed and said to those who followed him, "Truly I tell you, in no one in Israel have I found such faith. 11 I tell you, many will come from east and west and will eat with Abraham and Isaac and Jacob in the kingdom of heaven, 12 while the heirs of the kingdom will be thrown into the outer darkness, where there will be weeping and gnashing of teeth." 13 And to the centurion Jesus said, "Go; let it be done for you according to your faith." And the servant was healed in that hour.

Matthew 8:5–13 (NRSV)[1]
(See also Luke 7:1–10; John 4:46–54)

## Scholarly Context

As briefly indicated in chapter 1, the Two-Document Hypothesis postulates that the evangelists Matthew and Luke directly made independent use of Mark's Gospel as their primary source. In addition, they also drew from a common written Greek source consisting predominantly of a collection of

---

1. The pericope of Matthew 8:5–13, or Matthew 8:5–17, is liturgically read on the twelfth week Saturday Mass of Ordinary Time.

the sayings of Jesus, minimal narrative settings, parables, and two miracle stories. Scholars employ the siglum "Q," which is an abbreviation for the German word *Quelle*, meaning "source," to dub this non-Markan source.[2] Raymond E. Brown estimates that the "Q" source is roughly made of 220–235 verses shared in common by the Gospels of Matthew and Luke, which have no counterpart in Mark's Gospel.[3] These "Q" verses, inferred or reconstructed from the Gospels of Matthew and Luke, have strong verbal agreement and relative sequence. They are usually referred to by scholars as the Double Tradition (e.g., Matt 4:2b–11a || Luke 4:2–13; Matt 6:9–13 || Luke 11:2–4; Matt 18:12–14 || Luke 15:3–7; Matt 23:37–39 || Luke 13:34–35). The "Q" source may have come into existence before the Roman-Jewish War in 66–70 CE. As to a more precise date of composition and place of origin, Gerd Theissen postulates that it probably originated in Palestine in the forties and early fifties of the first century CE.[4]

The evangelist Matthew, who probably wrote the Gospel between 85–90 CE, has undoubtedly inherited from "Q" the pericope of the healing of the centurion's sick servant. It is the only expanded "Q" healing-miracle story he shares with the evangelist Luke (Luke 7:1–10). The Johannine pericope of the healing of the royal official's sick son (John 4:46–54) bears some striking resemblances to, and has some intriguing differences from, the healing of the centurion's sick servant in the "Q" tradition (Matt 8:5–13 || Luke 7:1–10). Scholars, however, are quite divided over whether "Q" and John are variant accounts derived from what appears to be the same traditional event, or are two separate and distinct incidents in Jesus' life.[5] For example, Hendrik van der Loos opines that Matthew 8:5–13, Luke 7:1–10, and John 4:46–54 are clearly recounting the same single event,[6] while Edward F. Siegman rejects the thesis that only one incident lies behind these three pericopae.[7]

2. See further Streeter, *Four Gospels*, 271–92; Vassiliadis, "Nature and Extent," 49–73; Kloppenborg, *Excavating Q*, 11–38; Kloppenborg, *Q, the Earliest Gospel*, 1–61; Tuckett, *Q and the History of Early Christianity*, 1–39.

3. See Brown, *Introduction to the New Testament*, 117.

4. See Theissen, *Shadow of the Galilean*, 189–90; Theissen, *Gospels in Context*, 221–34; Theissen and Merz, *Historical Jesus*, 27–29.

5. See further Dodd, *Historical Tradition*, 188–95; Meier, *Marginal Jew*, 2:718–26; Davies and Allison, *Critical and Exegetical Commentary*, 2:17–18; Bird, *Jesus and the Origins*, 116–21.

6. See Loos, *Miracles of Jesus*, 530–32; cf. Dunn, *Jesus Remembered*, 1:215–16.

7. See Siegman, "St. John's Use," 194; cf. Morris, *Gospel According to Matthew*, 191.

Having established a source behind the Matthean pericope of the healing of the centurion's sick servant, a juxtaposition with its Lukan version reveals some significant facts. There are several similarities worth mentioning. Both are virtually consistent in (1) placing the pericope immediately after Jesus' Sermon on the Mount (Matt 5:1—8:1) or on the Plain (Luke 6:17–49); (2) locating the setting of the pericope in Capernaum (Matt 8:5; Luke 7:1); (3) identifying the petitioner as a centurion, viz., a military commander (Matt 8:5, 8, 9, 13; Luke 7:2, 6, 8); (4) implying that the petitioner's ethnic identity is that of a gentile, viz., a non-Jew (Matt 8:9–10; Luke 7:9–8); (5) mentioning the centurion's request for the healing of his servant/slave (Matt 8:8; Luke 7:7); (6) having the centurion addressing Jesus as Κύριε (Kyrie, "Lord," "sir," Matt 8:6, 8; Luke 7:6); (7) emphasizing the unworthiness of the centurion, as well as his confidence in Jesus' healing power (Matt 8:8; Luke 7:6b–7); (8) referring to Jesus' amazement at the centurion's faith in contrast to Israel (Matt 8:10; Luke 7:9); (9) relating the exact verbal exchange between the centurion and Jesus (Matt 8:8–10; Luke 7:6b–9); and (10) reporting an instantaneous healing of the patient from a distance (Matt 8:13; Luke 7:10).

Despite these similarities, however, there are substantial differences between the Matthean and Lukan pericopae that deserve some attention. First, in Matthew's version, the centurion himself approaches Jesus personally to appeal on behalf of his sick servant (Matt 8:5–6), while in Luke's version, he has no direct contact at all with Jesus, but instead sends two separate delegations at two different times to intercede before Jesus on behalf of his sick slave—the first one consists of Jewish elders (Luke 7:3b) and the second one is comprised of friends (Luke 7:6a). Some scholars attribute the lack of the double-delegation motif from the Matthean pericope to the editorial activity of the evangelist himself.[8] R. T. France suggests that Matthew's deliberate omission "is a valid literary device to throw the emphasis clearly onto the central theme of the story, the centurion's faith."[9] This may well be true, given the fact that Matthew has a proclivity to abbreviate his Markan source material by omitting superfluous details. For example, he entirely drops from Mark 5:35 all mention of messengers coming to inform Jairus of the death of his little daughter (Matt 9:18–19,

---

8. See, for example, Davies and Allison, *Critical and Exegetical Commentary*, 2:19–20; Morris, *Gospel According to Matthew*, 191; Gundry, *Matthew*, 141, 147; Keener, *Gospel of Matthew*, 264; Osborne, *Matthew*, 289.

9. France, "Exegesis in Practice," 254.

23–26). However, Robert A. J. Gagnon convincingly argues that the linguistic vocabulary and style of the double-delegation motif (Luke 7:3b–6a) should be credited to Luke's redactional work.[10]

Second, Matthew and Luke are quite different in their description of the patient as well as the illness. Matthew overwhelmingly uses παῖς (*pais*) to refer to the patient of whom the centurion is worried (Matt 8:6, 8, 13). This is an ambiguous term that could imply the meaning of a "child," "son," "boy," or "servant."[11] Luke, on the other hand, predominantly employs δοῦλος (*doulos*), a term which literally means "slave" (Luke 7:2, 3, 8, 10[12]), but can also be metaphorically translated as "servant" (cf. Rom 1:1; Gal 1:10; Phil 1:1). Remarkably enough, while Luke has the centurion referring to his sick δοῦλος (*doulos*) as παῖς (*pais*, Luke 7:7), Matthew has the centurion alluding probably to his sick παῖς (*pais*) as δοῦλος (*doulos*, Matt 8:9). Matthew identifies the illness from which the patient is grievously suffering as paralysis (Matt 8:6), while Luke only mentions that the centurion's slave is ill and at the point of death, without specifying the cause of the illness (Luke 7:2).[13]

Finally, in contrast to Luke 7:1–10, the Matthean pericope of the healing of the centurion's sick servant contains an authentic twofold logion of Jesus about an eschatological pronouncement concerning the inclusion of "many" (gentiles) and the exclusion of "the sons" (Jews) into and from the kingdom of heaven (Matt 8:11–12). This logion of Jesus, which belongs to the "Q" tradition, is also found in a different context and reverse order in Luke 13:28–29 (Matt 8:11 = Luke 13:29; Matt 8:12 = Luke 13:28).[14] While many scholars are convinced that Matthew is responsible for the insertion of the logion of Jesus into the pericope of the healing of the centurion's sick servant (Matt 8:5–10 [11–12], 13),[15] Edward

10. See further Gagnon, "Statistical Analysis," 709–31; Gagnon, "Luke's Motives," 122–45; Gagnon, "Shape of Matthew's Q," 133–42; cf. Fitzmyer, *Gospel According to Luke I–IX*, 649.

11. See *BDAG*, 750.

12. See *BDAG*, 259–60.

13. See Schweizer, *Good News According to Matthew*, 212; Nolland, *Gospel of Matthew*, 354.

14. See further Davies and Allison, *Critical and Exegetical Commentary*, 2:26; Meier, *Marginal Jew*, 2:309–17; Siker, *Disinheriting the Jews*, 82–85; Bird, *Jesus and the Origins*, 83–93; Bird, *Gospel of Lord*, 171–74.

15. See Bultmann, *History of the Synoptic Tradition*, 38; Meier, *Matthew*, 84; Meier, *Marginal Jew*, 2:309–10; Siker, *Disinheriting the Jews*, 84; Harrington, *Gospel of Matthew*,

Schweizer suggests that it possibly belonged from the very beginning to the pericope and "may well have been uttered under circumstances like those described"[16] in Matthew 8:5–13.

On the whole, the presence of possible elements of Matthean and Lukan editorial activity patently demonstrates that each evangelist has evidently treated the material found in the "Q" source quite differently in order to make it fit into the overall theological and literary context of his Gospel narrative. Putting these differences aside, some scholars have judged Matthew's terse version to be substantially closer to the "Q" tradition than Luke's lengthy and verbose version.[17]

## Literary Genre and Structure

The form of the pericope of the healing of the centurion's sick servant in Matthew 8:5–13 obviously defies any conventional and neat form-critical categories. In fact, it has been classified and, consequently, treated as an apophthegm,[18] a pronouncement story,[19] a story about Jesus,[20] and a miracle story.[21] The pericope, as it stands, can be plainly viewed as an apophthegmatic healing-miracle story,[22] which has certain affinities to the pericope of the exorcism of the Canaanite woman's daughter (Matt 15:21–28 ‖ Mark 7:24–30). Although the pericope begins with the centurion's implied request for the physical healing of his servant (Matt 8:6) and ends with Jesus' granting the centurion's request (Matt 8:13), the miracle

---

116; Davies and Allison, *Critical and Exegetical Commentary*, 2:25; Gundry, *Matthew*, 145; Schnackenburg, *Gospel of Matthew*, 82; France, "Exegesis in Practice," 253–54, 260; France, *Gospel of Matthew*, 310; Nolland, *Gospel of Matthew*, 353; Evans, *Matthew*, 190; Luz, *Matthew 8–20*, 9; Fitzmyer, *Gospel According to Luke I–IX*, 649.

16. Schweizer, *Good News According to Matthew*, 213; see also Osborne, *Matthew*, 288–89.

17. See Derrett, "Law in the New Testament," 174; Fitzmyer, *Gospel According to Luke I–IX*, 648–49; Walaskay, *'And so We Came to Rome,'* 32; Fleddermann, *Q*, 337; Luz, *Matthew 8–20*, 8.

18. See Bultmann, *History of the Synoptic Tradition*, 38–39.

19. See Fitzmyer, *Gospel According to Luke I–IX*, 649; Davies and Allison, *Critical and Exegetical Commentary*, 2:17.

20. See Taylor, *Formation of the Gospel Tradition*, 75–76.

21. See Theissen, *Gospels in Context*, 226; Theissen, *Miracle Stories*, 254; Meier, *Marginal Jew*, 2:718.

22. See Luz, *Matthew 8–20*, 8; Catchpole, *Quest for Q*, 281; Kloppenborg, *Formation of Q*, 118; Keener, *Gospel of Matthew*, 246.

itself is completely subordinated to the dialogue (Matt 8:8–10), as well as to the twofold logion of Jesus (Matt 8:11–12), which are ultimately the outstanding features of the pericope. There is no doubt that the dialogue between the centurion and Jesus is inextricably connected with, and leads to, the physical healing of the centurion's servant.[23] By inserting Matthew 8:11–12 into the pericope, the evangelist has added an apophthegmatic character to the "Q" healing-miracle story.

The present pericope contains the basic threefold pattern of a healing-miracle story. First, the *description of disease* contains a brief diagnosis of the sufferer's illness: the centurion's servant suffers from paralysis (Matt 8:6). Second, the *healing of disease* shows that the sufferer's illness is solely healed by the miracle-worker: Jesus utters his authoritative word, which effects the healing the centurion has requested (Matt 8:13a). Third, the *proof of healing* provides at least some evidence, which verifies the success of the miracle itself: the centurion's servant is healed at once (Matt 8:13b). Furthermore, there are at least eight literary motifs embedded in the pericope, which also appear in ancient Jewish, Hellenistic, and Greco-Roman healing miracle stories.[24] They are as follows:

1. The Coming of the Miracle-Worker ("Having he now entered into Capernaum," Matt 8:5a).

2. The Appearance of Representatives (". . . a centurion came to him," Matt 8:5b).

3. Description of the Distress ("Lord, my servant has been thrown down in the house, paralyzed and grievously tormented," Matt 8:6).

4. Difficulties in the Approach ("Shall I come heal him?" Matt 8:7).

5. Pleas and Expressions of Trust ("Lord, I am not worthy that you should come under my roof, but only speak the word, and my servant will be healed," Matt 8:8).

6. Assurance (". . . be it happen to you as you have believed," Matt 8:13a).

7. Recognition of the Miracle (". . . and the servant was healed in that hour," Matt 8:13b).

8. Dismissal ("Go," Matt 8:13a).

23. See Luz, *Matthew 8–20*, 8.
24. See Theissen, *Miracle Stories*, 47–72.

The literary structure of the pericope seems to unfold in a series of six scenes: (1) introductory setting (Matt 8:5a), (2) the centurion's arrival and implied request (Matt 8:5b–6), (3) Jesus' response (Matt 8:7), (4) the centurion's counterresponse (Matt 8:8–9), (5) Jesus' reaction and declaration (Matt 8:10–12), and (6) assurance and immediacy of healing (Matt 8:13).

## Narrative Analysis

### Introductory Setting (Matt 8:5a)

One can deduce with certainty from both Matthean and Lukan context and sequence that the pericope of the healing of the centurion's servant/slave immediately followed Jesus' Sermon on the Mount/Plain and took place in the locality of Capernaum in its "Q" source. However, one can still identify some skillful editorial touches from Matthew's own pen. In contrast to Luke, Matthew interrupts the "Q" sequence by inserting the Markan pericope of Jesus' healing of the leper (Matt 8:2–4 ‖ Mark 1:40–45) between Jesus' Sermon on the Mount (Matt 5:1—8:1) and Jesus' healing of the centurion's servant (Matt 8:5–13).[25] Thus, putting aside Matthew 4:23–25 (cf. Mark 1:39), which is a summary statement encapsulating Jesus' teaching, preaching, and healing programmatic ministry in Galilee, the "Q" pericope of the centurion's servant in Capernaum becomes the second healing-miracle story recorded in Matthew's Gospel, whose recipient, like the first healing-miracle story of the leper, is an anonymous minor character.

The evangelist begins the pericope with a collocation of a genitive absolute participle followed by an adversative particle, a pronoun, and a preposition: Εἰσελθόντος δὲ αὐτοῦ εἰς Καφαρναοὺμ (Eiselthontos de autou eis Kapharnaoum, "Having he now entered into Capernaum," Matt 8:5a). This grammatical construction, particularly the use of the participial genitive absolute at the beginning of a sentence, is a characteristic feature of Matthew's writing style (e.g., Matt 2:1; 8:1, 28; 14:32; 17:9, 22, 24; 20:29; 24:3; 26:6; 27:19).[26] Furthermore, the evangelist's habitual use of a postpositive particle δὲ (de, "but," "now") in Matthew 8:5a seems to introduce a shift in the narrative scene and setting by separating Matthew 8:2–4 from Matthew

25. See Harrington, Gospel of Matthew, 112; Gundry, Matthew, 140–41; Davies and Allison, Critical and Exegetical Commentary, 2:17; Evans, Matthew, 185–86.

26. See Gundry, Matthew, 141; Davies and Allison, Critical and Exegetical Commentary, 2:18; Fleddermann, Q, 336.

8:5b–13. In the former, Jesus encounters and heals the leper apparently out-side Capernaum, while in the latter he encounters the centurion and heals his sick servant at a distance obviously inside Capernaum.

Καφαρναοὺμ (*Kapharnaoum*) is a Greek rendering of the Hebrew כְּפַר נַחוּם (*kĕfar-naḥûm*, "village of Nachum," "village of consolation"). Despite its frequent mention in the Gospels, about sixteen times, Capernaum never appears in the Hebrew Bible. The first-century Jewish historian Josephus, however, calls it a village (*Life* 72 §§402–3) and describes its natural and agricultural beauty (*J.W.* 3.10.8 §§516–21). At the time of Jesus, it is esti-mated that the size of Capernaum's population "would have been between 600 and 1,200 inhabitants."[27] This might be one of the reasons why Jesus moved his place of residence from his hometown Nazareth (Matt 2:22–23), a village with fewer than 400 residents, to Capernaum, making the latter the central headquarters for his Galilean ministry (Matt 4:13; 9:1). Caper-naum is today identified with Tell Ḥûm on the northwest shore of the Sea of Galilee. Two important archaeological sites were discovered at this Jewish fishing village: the remains of a large room that was probably part of Simon Peter's house (Matt 8:14; 17:24–25) and the ruins of a fourth-century CE white limestone synagogue, which has underneath it a visible black basalt stone foundation probably belonging to a synagogue the centurion built in Capernaum (cf. Mark 1:21; Luke 4:31–33; 7:5; John 6:59).[28]

### The Centurion's Arrival and Implied Request (Matt 8:5b–6)

After Jesus' entry into Capernaum, a new and anonymous character im-mediately enters the scene with a reverential attitude and a great sense of exigency. He is introduced by his Greek military title: ἑκατόνταρχος (*heka-tontarchos*, "centurion," "captain," Matt 8:5b, 8, 13[29]). As the word indicates, he would have ethnically been a gentile centurion commanding a single infantry unit, roughly containing up to 100 non-Jewish soldiers. Further-more, he would have most likely been a Syrian, not Roman, citizen in the service of Herod Antipas, tetrarch of Galilee and Perea (Matt 14:1; Luke 3:9; *Ant.* 17.8.1 §118; however, Matt 14:9 and Mark 6:14 refer to him as "king"),

---

27. Reed, *Archaeology and the Galilean Jesus*, 152.

28. See further Corbo, "Capernaum," 866–68; Murphy-O'Connor, *Holy Land*, 250–54; Rousseau and Arav, *Jesus and His World*, 39–47; Safrai, "Synagogue the Centurion Built," 12–14; Theissen and Merz, *Historical Jesus*, 167.

29. See *BDAG*, 298–99.

who, just like his father, Herod the Great (*Ant.* 17.8.3 §§198–99), employed non-Jewish soldiers. As a puppet of Rome, Herod Antipas served Roman interests. He probably had a small garrison stationed in Capernaum because it was a customs station (Matt 9:9) and a frontier geopolitical village adjacent to the territory of his half-brother, Herod Philip.[30] Herod Antipas had John the Baptist arrested, imprisoned, and executed in the fortress of Machaerus (Matt 14:1–12; Mark 6:14–29; Luke 9:7–9; *Ant.* 18.5.2 §§116–19). Jesus derisively calls him "a fox" (Luke 13:32).

Intriguingly, all centurions mentioned in the New Testament, for example, the centurion at Capernaum ("Q" = Matt 8:5–13 ‖ Luke 7:1–10), the centurion at Jesus' crucifixion scene in Jerusalem (Mark 15:39 ‖ Matt 27:54 ‖ Luke 23:47), Cornelius at Caesarea (Acts 10:1–2), the centurion who informs his commander that Paul is a Roman citizen (Acts 22:25–26), and Julius who saves Paul's life on the trip to Rome (Acts 27:1, 43), are favorably portrayed.

News of Jesus' charismatic ministry of teaching, preaching, and healing in Galilee spreads throughout Syria (Matt 4:23–24), a region northeast of the Sea of Galilee predominantly inhabited by non-Jewish populations. The centurion must have heard of Jesus' growing reputation and popularity as a miracle-worker (cf. Luke 7:3). Impelled by dire necessity, he προσῆλθεν αὐτῷ . . . παρακαλῶν αὐτὸν (*prosēlthen autō . . . parakalōn auton,* "approached him . . . imploring him," Matt 8:5b), a gesture connoting his deferential attitude toward Jesus. Moreover, the evangelist categorically heightens the majesty, sublimity, and dignity of Jesus by his quite frequent use of the verb προσέρχεσθαι (*proserchesthai,* "to approach," "to come to"[31]) to speak of various characters approaching Jesus for different reasons, such as the tempter (Matt 4:3), angels (Matt 4:11), disciples (Matt 5:1), a leper (Matt 8:2), a centurion (Matt 8:5), a scribe (Matt 8:19), disciples of John (Matt 9:14), a bleeding woman (Matt 9:20), two blind men (Matt 9:28), Pharisees and scribes (Matt 15:1), Pharisees and Sadducees (Matt 16:1), a man whose son suffers from epilepsy (Matt 17:14), Peter (Matt 18:21), the mother of James and John (Matt 20:20), blind and lame people (Matt 21:14),

---

30. See further Meier, *Matthew,* 83; Meier, *Marginal Jew,* 2:720–21; Schnackenburg, *Gospel of Matthew,* 82; Harrington, *Gospel of Matthew,* 113; Schweizer, *Good News According to Matthew,* 213; Morris, *Gospel According to Matthew,* 192; Evans, *Matthew,* 187; Gundry, *Matthew,* 141; France, "Exegesis in Practice," 255; France, *Gospel of Matthew,* 311; Nolland, *Gospel of Matthew,* 354; Dunn, *Jesus Remembered,* 1:310; Reed, *Archaeology and the Galilean Jesus,* 161–62; Theissen and Merz, *Historical Jesus,* 166.

31. See *BDAG,* 878.

chief priests and the elders (Matt 21:23), and a woman with an alabaster jar (Matt 26:7). The use of the verb παρακαλεῖν (*parakalein*, "to implore," "to request," "to entreat," Matt 8:5[32]) discloses the centurion's vulnerability and feeling of helplessness. It also plays a significant part in imparting a heightened sense of urgency to the pericope.

Having come face to face with Jesus himself, the centurion addresses him as Κύριε (*Kyrie*, "Lord," "sir," Matt 8:6, 8). Used in the vocative form (Matt 7:21–22; 8:2, 21, 25; 9:28; 14:28, 30; 15:22, 25, 27; 16:22; 17:4, 15; 18:21; 20:30–31; 25:37, 44), this word is not a mere secular and courteous title, but an honorific designation denoting the centurion's subordination to Jesus' authority and superiority (cf. Matt 27:63).[33] Remarkably, Jesus' opponents never greet or address him with such an appellation in Matthew's Gospel. However, those who approach Jesus in Matthew's Gospel "uttering the word *kyrie*," writes Jack D. Kingsbury, "are doing so in acknowledgment of the divine authority with which Jesus the Messiah heals (8:1–4, 5–13; 17:14–18), saves (8:23–27), and teaches (8:21–22; 16:21–23; 18:21–22)."[34]

With respect to the centurion's statement that his servant βέβληται ἐν τῇ οἰκίᾳ παραλυτικός, δεινῶς βασανιζόμενος (*beblētai en tē oikia paralytikos, deinōs basanizomenos*, "has been thrown down in the house, paralyzed and grievously tormented," Matt 8:6), there is no specific petition for healing, but only a description of the servant's malady and dreadful condition. Nevertheless, certain underlying points stand out distinctly from it. First, it clearly identifies the affliction as paralysis (cf. Matt 4:24; 9:2, 6; Mark 2:3–5, 9–10; Acts 8:7) and emphasizes the acuteness and severity of the physical pain and mental distress of the centurion's servant. The affliction of paralysis—a loss of muscle function probably caused by a sudden spinal cord injury—has smitten and thrown the servant down (cf. Matt 8:14; 9:2, 6; Acts 9:33). Second, it transparently reveals the centurion's genuine concern and care for the well-being of his servant (cf. Matt 9:2; 15:22; 17:15). He definitely wants him to be healed. Third, and even more fundamentally, it obliquely demonstrates the centurion's implied confidence in Jesus' therapeutic power, without making a direct request (cf. Matt 8:14–15).

---

32. See *BDAG*, 764–65.

33. See Harrington, *Gospel of Matthew*, 113; France, "Exegesis in Practice," 255; Osborne, *Matthew*, 290.

34. Kingsbury, "Title 'Kyrios' in Matthew's Gospel," 254.

It is noteworthy to mention at this juncture that the encounter between Jesus, a Jew, and the centurion, a gentile (Hebrew: גּוֹי [gôy][35]; Greek: ἐθνικός [ethnikos][36]), in the largely Jewish village of Capernaum, is unprecedented. It is the first time that the adult Jesus comes into direct contact with a gentile in the narrative framework of Matthew's Gospel. In retrospect, the magi who travel from the east, probably from Babylon (cf. Isa 47:13; Dan 2:2), all the way to Jerusalem, then to Bethlehem to pay homage to the infant Jesus (Matt 2:1–12), are the first gentiles to have direct contact with the baby Jesus. They are positively depicted, apart from Joseph and Mary, as being the first to acknowledge the royal birth of the Jewish Messiah. Historically speaking, the Jewish-gentile relationship was conspicuously marked by strict demarcation (cf. 1 Macc 1:11–15). Jewish religious beliefs, dietary restrictions, and purity laws, such as belief in one God (Deut 6:4; Isa 44:6), practice of circumcision (Gen 17:10–11; Luke 2:21; *Hist.* 5:5), possession of Torah (Deut 4:40; Rom 2; Gal 2:15), observance of the Sabbath (Exod 20:8–11; Deut 5:12–15), refusal to eat pork (Lev 11:7; Deut 8:14; *Ag. Ap.* 2.14 §§137–41), and prohibition against marrying a gentile woman (Deut 7:3–4; *Ant.* 8.7.5 §191), restricted contact between Jews and gentiles, and, consequently, served as boundary markers and barriers, separating observant Jews from their gentile neighbors.[37] This demarcation seems to be evident even in the Sermon on the Mount. Prior to his encounter with the centurion, Jesus utilizes two oppositional plural terms οἱ ἐθνικοὶ (*hoi ethnikoi*, Matt 5:47; 6:7) and τὰ ἔθνη (*ta ethnē*, Matt 6:32), both meaning "the gentiles," as a negative foil group to highlight characteristics of the ideal disciples (Matt 5:47; 6:7–8, 31–33). How would Jesus then respond to the centurion's implied request in Matthew 8:6?

## *Jesus' Response (Matt 8:7)*

The evangelist employs the vivid historical present tense λέγει (*legei*, "he says," Matt 8:7a) to introduce and emphasize Jesus' authoritative word (e.g., Matt 4:10; 8:4; 9:6; 12:13; 14:31; 15:34; 17:20; 18:22; 19:18; 20:21; 21:13; 22:20; 26:64; 28:10). The key issue is whether Jesus' initial response to the centurion in Matthew 8:7b expresses assent or dissent. There is at present

35. See *BDB*, 156.

36. See *BDAG*, 276.

37. For the relationship of the Jews to gentiles, see further Cohen, *From the Maccabees to the Mishnah*, 27–59.

no consensus among scholars and Bible English translations on how to precisely translate the Greek clause Ἐγὼ ἐλθὼν θεραπεύσω αὐτόν (*Egō elthōn therapeusō auton*, Matt 8:7b). It is grammatically possible to render it in two different ways. It can be punctuated as a statement, "I, coming, I will heal him," denoting Jesus' openness, willingness, readiness, and eagerness to heal the centurion's servant.[38] KJV, NASB, and RSV translate it as "I will come and heal him," while JB renders it as "I will come myself and cure him." However, it can also be punctuated as a question, "I, coming, will I heal him?" connoting indignation, hesitancy, aloofness, and rebuff on the part of Jesus.[39] Thus, the NIV translates it as "Shall I come and heal him?" while CSB renders it as "Am I to come and heal him?"

It is probably best to rhetorically construe Jesus' initial response as an astonished and indignant question, provoking and testing the centurion to enter into a dialogue and reveal the depth of his faith by moving from his implicit confidence to explicit expression of total trust in Jesus. There seems to be some evidence in support of such a reading. First, the future verb θεραπεύσω (*therapeusō*) contains its pronoun subject in its ending: "I will heal." However, the additional use and placement of the first-person singular pronoun Ἐγὼ (*Egō*, "I") at the very beginning of the sentence is emphatic, requiring Jesus' response to be construed as a question.

Second, and in connection with the previous point, the centurion has already informed Jesus that his servant is at home, suffering from excruciating paralysis. Jesus understands the centurion's implied request as an inappropriate invitation to come and enter into his residence and heal his sick servant. His response, therefore, expresses reluctance to consent. It seems that Palestinian Jews did not enter a gentile dwelling for fear of ritual defilement (Matt 10:5–6; John 18:28–29; Acts 10:28; *J.W.* 2.2.10 §150; *m.* 'Ohal. 18:7). It is interesting to note that the Gospels never depict Jesus entering a gentile house. They, however, portray him journeying through largely gentile

38. See Schweizer, *Good News According to Matthew*, 213; Schnackenburg, *Gospel of Matthew*, 82; Meier, *Matthew*, 83; Meier, *Marginal Jew*, 2:719; Gundry, *Matthew*, 143; Derrett, "Law in the New Testament," 175–76; Fleddermann, *Q*, 350–51; Catchpole, *Quest for Q*, 289–92.

39. See McNeile, *Gospel According to St. Matthew*, 104; Bultmann, *History of the Synoptic Tradition*, 38; Harrington, *Gospel of Matthew*, 113; Morris, *Gospel According to Matthew*, 192–93; Evans, *Matthew*, 187; Keener, *Gospel of Matthew*, 266; Davies and Allison, *Critical and Exegetical Commentary*, 2:21–22; Nolland, *Gospel of Matthew*, 354–55; Talbert, *Matthew*, 113; France, "Exegesis in Practice," 256–57; France, *Gospel of Matthew*, 312–13; Osborne, *Matthew*, 290; Siegman, "St. John's Use," 185; Loos, *Miracles of Jesus*, 533–34; Levine, "Matthew's Advice," 30; Luz, *Matthew 8–20*, 10.

territories where some of his miracles and teachings take place (e.g., Matt 8:28–34 || Mark 5:1–20 || Luke 8:26–39; Matt 15:21–28 || Mark 7:24–30; Mark 7:31–37; Matt 15:32–39 || Mark 8:1–10; Matt 16:13–20 || Mark 8:27–30 || Luke 9:18–20). Therefore, Jesus' response may be tendentiously rendered as a question, meaning: "Shall I, a Jew, come to your residence, a gentile, to heal your sick servant?" It is clear that "Matthew is concerned," writes Ulrich Luz, "to demonstrate that Jesus is faithful to the law."[40]

Third, the centurion's humble counterresponse to Jesus (Matt 8:8–9), called forth by Jesus' dissent, makes the dialogue flow naturally and smoothly, leading up to an unexpected emotional reaction on the part of Jesus, viz., his amazement at the depth of the centurion's faith (Matt 8:10). Faith, on the part of the suppliant, defuses racial tension because it unambiguously exhibits the centurion's trust and confidence in Jesus to accomplish what he has desired. This element, viz., the boldness of faith, recalls Jesus' encounter with a Canaanite woman whose daughter he heals from her demonic possession, after his expression of initial resistance and reluctance. The healing takes place at a distance in the non-Jewish neighborhood of Tyre and Sidon (Matt 15:21–28 || Mark 7:24–30). In both pericopae, the faith of either the centurion or the Canaanite woman overcomes the apparent obstacle of reluctance, "proving stronger than the racial barrier," writes R. T. France, "and in each case Jesus then effects the cure in explicit response to this faith."[41]

Remarkably, all the individualized gentile characters who come into explicit contact with Jesus, such as the magi from the east (Matt 2:1–12), the centurion at Galilee (Matt 8:5–13), the Canaanite woman from the region of Tyre and Sidon (Matt 15:21–28), and the Roman centurion and soldiers in Jerusalem (Matt 27:54), are positively portrayed in Matthew's Gospel as exemplars and paradigms of faith and their stories anticipate the Great Commission at the conclusion of the Gospel (Matt 28:16–20).[42] Faith in Jesus, viz., recognition of his royalty, authority, messiahship, and divine sonship, brings an end to cultural tension between Jews and gentiles (cf. Rom 11:11–12; 1 Cor 10:32–33; Gal 2:15–21; Eph 2:11–22).

40. Luz, *Matthew 8–20*, 10.

41. France, "Exegesis in Practice," 257.

42. See further Senior, "Between Two Worlds," 1–23.

## The Centurion's Counterresponse (Matt 8:8–9)

Jesus' extraordinary response to the centurion elicits an equally extraordinary counterresponse from the centurion. Like John the Baptist before him (Matt 3:11), the centurion unreservedly humbles himself and acknowledges his inferior status to Jesus. His self-abasing statement, Κύριε, οὐκ εἰμὶ ἱκανός (*Kyrie, ouk eimi hikanos,* "Lord, I am not worthy," Matt 8:8a), profoundly underscores his own sense of unworthiness to have Jesus come under the roof of his dwelling and heal his sick servant, thus demonstrating, in part, respect for first-century Jewish practice of avoiding entering a gentile house lest one incurred ritual defilement. Perhaps even more importantly, the centurion's feeling of inadequacy stems from his personal recognition of Jesus as a Galilean, holy, charismatic miracle-worker and faith-healer, whose authoritative word has power over disease. He is cognizant of the unparalleled "majesty and authority of Jesus which lift him above everything human, especially in the non-Jewish sphere."[43] Up to this point in the Gospel narrative, Jesus' public ministry is proof of his majesty and authority (e.g., Matt 4:23–25; 7:28–29; 8:1–4).

The centurion is wholeheartedly confident that Jesus' authoritative word has the ability to restore his sick servant to the fullness of life, even from a distance. He thus deems the coming of Jesus to his residence in order to get physically close to his paralyzed servant as an unnecessary step. All he is asking him at this moment is to issue a single miracle-working word to accomplish healing: ἀλλὰ μόνον εἰπὲ λόγῳ, καὶ ἰαθήσεται ὁ παῖς μου (*alla monon eipe logō, kai iathēsetai ho pais mou,* "but only say a word and my servant will be cured," Matt 8:8b). Note that Matthew uses two verbs in this pericope to describe physical healing—θεραπεύειν (*therapeuein,* "to heal," Matt 8:7b) and ἰᾶσθαι (*iasthai,* "to cure," Matt 8:8b, 13)—without a difference in meaning.

The centurion acknowledges that a disease such as paralysis is subject to Jesus' authoritative word, just as the centurion's subordinates are subject to his military dictates. The centurion's words ultimately show and express the full extent of his faith in Jesus. Having revealed the depth of his faith, he speaks of himself as being a military man ὑπὸ ἐξουσίαν (*hypo exousian,* "under authority," Matt 8:9). His own authority is solely derived from his superiors, namely Herod Antipas and Tiberius Caesar Augustus. Being under authority certainly warrants him to have authority

---

43. Rengstorf, "ἱκανός, ἱκανότης, ἱικανόω," 294.

45

and, consequently, exercise it over his inferiors, namely soldiers, servants, and slaves. He employs a triad of imperative verbs (Πορεύθητι, *Poreuthēti* ["Go"], Ἔρχου, *Erchou* ["Come"], and Ποίησον τοῦτο, *Poiēson touto* ["Do this"], Matt 8:9) to demonstrate how his subordinates obediently carry out his directives without question or hesitation.

The centurion's intention is twofold. On the one hand, just as he is capable of exercising authority over military personnel who unquestionably obey his orders, so is Jesus competent to exercise power over disease; and his authoritative word undoubtedly effects the healing of the body and mind of the paralyzed servant, even from a distance. Both the centurion and Jesus are men vested with authority: the former by the tetrarchial and imperial authority of Herod Antipas and Tiberius Caesar Augustus, and the latter by divine authority of the God of Israel (cf. Matt 11:27; 28:18). On the other hand, the centurion's finite authority stands in stark contrast to Jesus' infinite authority. He has no power to deliver his servant from his agonizing paralysis. He, therefore, has come to Jesus, with humility and faith, knowing that, through him, God's therapeutic power extends beyond the boundaries of race and distance. Harry T. Fleddermann puts it well when he writes, "Although the centurion has real power, he cannot cure, he cannot save his servant from the human condition. In his humility he recognizes that he stands face to face with absolute power."[44]

## Jesus' Reaction and Declaration (Matt 8:10–12)

The positive counterresponse of the centurion definitely generates a positive reaction from Jesus himself. Matthew preserves a description from "Q," capturing Jesus' emotional state: ἀκούσας δὲ ὁ Ἰησοῦς ἐθαύμασεν (*akousas de ho Iēsous ethaumasen*, "but Jesus, having heard, marveled," Matt 8:10). The verb θαυμάζειν (*thaumazein*, "to wonder," "to be astonished," "to be amazed"[45]) is employed only twice in the Gospels with Jesus being its subject—once by "Q" to describe Jesus' astonishment at the faith of the gentile centurion (Matt 8:10 ‖ Luke 7:9), and once by the evangelist Mark to relate Jesus' amazement at the lack of faith of the Jewish inhabitants of his hometown Nazareth (Mark 6:6). It is usually used in the Gospels to describe the extraordinary reactions of people, whether advocates or opponents, to the

---

44. Fleddermann, Q, 351.

45. See *BDAG*, 444–45.

person, words, and deeds of Jesus (e.g., Matt 8:27; 9:33; 15:31; 21:20; 22:22; 27:14; Mark 5:20; Luke 4:22; 11:38; John 7:15).

Impressed by the centurion's faith, Jesus can hardly contain himself. He now addresses those following him, most likely Simon Peter, Andrew, James, and John (Matt 4:18–22), as well as the large crowds (Matt 4:25; 5:1; 7:28; 8:1). He prefaces his saying with his own characteristic introductory formula Ἀμὴν λέγω ὑμῖν (Amēn legō hymin, "Amen, I say to you [plural]," Matt 8:10). This solemn formula, which occurs some thirty-one times in Matthew's Gospel (e.g., Matt 5:18; 6:2; 10:15; 11:11; 13:17; 16:28; 17:20; 18:3; 19:23; 21:21; 23:36; 24:2; 25:12; 26:13), is employed as a literary device to emphasize the significance of what follows. The prefatory Ἀμὴν (Amēn) is a Greek transliteration of the Hebrew אָמֵן (ʾāmēn), meaning "truly" or "verily."[46] It functions as an asseverative particle.[47] The subject of Jesus' marvel is the quality of the centurion's faith: παρ᾽ οὐδενὶ τοσαύτην πίστιν ἐν τῷ Ἰσραὴλ εὗρον (par᾽ oudeni tosautēn pistin en tō Israēl heuron, "with no one in Israel I have found faith so great," Matt 8:10). Here, faith clearly does not allude to a body of essential doctrine one needs to acknowledge to be true; but it rather refers to the centurion's audacious admission of trust and confidence that Jesus, as a miracle-worker, "could heal at a distance with a mere word and would do so even though asked by a gentile."[48] Such faith Jesus has never encountered among individual Israelites. He will later commend another gentile, a Canaanite woman, for her extraordinary faith (Matt 15:28). Both encounters and interactions with the centurion and the Canaanite woman apparently teach Jesus something about the bold humility and faith of gentiles. Consequently, he ends up granting both requests for healing.

At this juncture, Matthew redactionally inserts an independent two-fold "Q" logion of Jesus (Matt 8:11–12) into the "Q" healing-miracle story (Matt 8:5–10, 13) to juxtapose between πολλοὶ (polloi, "many," Matt 8:11) and οἱ υἱοὶ τῆς βασιλείας (hoi huioi tēs basileias, "the sons of the kingdom," Matt 8:12). Note that Matthew 8:11 is a promise, while Matthew 8:12 is a threat. The adversative δὲ (de, "but," Matt 8:11, 12) is employed twice to amplify this contrast.

It makes sense, given the context of the pericope, that the "many" who will come from east and west and recline at the eschatological festive

46. See *BDB*, 53.
47. See further Chilton, "Amen," 184–86.
48. Gundry, *Matthew*, 144.

banquet in the heavenly kingdom with the three founding fathers of Judaism—Abraham, his son Isaac, and his grandson Jacob—most likely refers to the gentiles.[49] However, W. D. Davies and Dale. C. Allison propose that "many" refers to unprivileged diasporic Jews who did not live in the land of Israel and, consequently, did not hear Jesus' message. They, not the gentiles, will find eschatological salvation.[50]

Jesus makes it clear that faith, not racial lineage, becomes the sole condition for the inclusion of gentiles into the kingdom of heaven. Faith in Jesus, which nullifies primal division and separation between Jews and gentiles, is an admission ticket, so to speak, into the kingdom of heaven. Consequently, there will be no disputes over ritual purity and impurity in the kingdom of heaven. Jesus' words in Matthew 8:11 imply that the faith of the centurion has granted him a place at the eschatological banquet.[51] There is a verbal agreement between Matthew 8:11 and Luke 13:29: they both employ the "Q" verb ἀνακλίνειν (anaklinein, "to recline," "to sit down"[52]) to describe the custom of reclining at a festive meal.

The Semitic expression, "the sons of the kingdom," refers to the Jewish people who naturally and rightfully are the recipients of Yahweh's blessings and promises, made available through Yahweh's covenants with Abraham, Isaac, and Jacob (cf. Matt 22:32). They belong to the kingdom. However, those who reject Jesus and his mission will suffer dire consequences. Thus, in sharp contrast to the image of many gentiles reclining at the eschatological festive banquet in the heavenly kingdom with the trio of patriarchs, they will be cast out from the kingdom into the outermost darkness, where they will experience weeping and grinding of teeth, even though they are the descendants of Abraham (Matt 3:9). This tragic exclusion from the kingdom of heaven is a typical Matthean description, signifying perdition (Matt 13:42, 50; 22:13; 24:51; 25:30).

---

49. See Harrington, *Gospel of Matthew*, 117; Schnackenburg, *Gospel of Matthew*, 82–83; Meier, *Matthew*, 84; Meier, *Marginal Jew*, 2:315; Schweizer, *Good News According to Matthew*, 214–15; Morris, *Gospel According to Matthew*, 195; Keener, *Gospel of Matthew*, 269; Gundry, *Matthew*, 145; France, "Exegesis in Practice," 261; Talbert, *Matthew*, 114; Osborne, *Matthew*, 293.

50. See Davies and Allison, *Critical and Exegetical Commentary*, 2:27–31.

51. See Meier, *Matthew*, 84; Gundry, *Matthew*, 145.

52. See *BDAG*, 65.

## Assurance and Immediacy of Healing (Matt 8:13)

The evangelist, having taken the liberty of relating the independent twofold "Q" logion of Jesus in Matthew 8:11–12, now returns in Matthew 8:13 to the story proper, which he resumes where he left off in Matthew 8:10.

By turning away from those following him and turning toward the centurion, Jesus now dismisses him with words of assurance, granting his request in response to faith: Ὕπαγε, ὡς ἐπίστευσας γενηθήτω σοι (*Hypage, hōs episteusas genēthētō soi*, "Go, be it happen to you as you have believed," Matt 8:13a). It is important to realize that there is an inextricable connection between faith in Jesus and immediacy of healing (e.g., Matt 9:1–8, 20–22, 27–31; 15:21–28). It is axiomatic that the faith that has caused Jesus to be astonished and, consequently, effected an immediate healing, is not that of the sick servant but of the centurion, who has confidently come to Jesus asking for intervention (cf. Matt 9:1–8; 15:21–28). Matthew concludes the pericope with the closing remarks, καὶ ἰάθη ὁ παῖς [αὐτοῦ] ἐν τῇ ὥρᾳ ἐκείνῃ (*kai iathē ho pais [autou] en tē hōra ekeinē*, "and the servant [his] was cured in that hour," Matt 8:13b), verifying that the instantaneous healing at a distance occurred at precisely the same time that Jesus pronounced his authoritative word of solace (cf. Matt 15:25; 17:18).

At this point, it is interesting to mention Rabbi Ḥanina ben Dosa, a first-century Galilean charismatic miracle-worker, whose intervention was sought in cases of illness. In the Babylonian Talmud, there are two consecutive miracle stories about his healing by prayer from a distance the son of Rabban Gamliel, who suffered from a fever, and the son of Rabbi Yoḥanan ben Zakkai, who fell ill (*b. Ber.* 34b). Both Rabbi Ḥanina and Jesus are accredited with having healed sick people from a distance. However, unlike Rabbi Ḥanina, who resorts to prayer and intercession to effect healing, Jesus is described as having healed in virtue of his own authoritative word; he does what only God of Israel can do. In other words, as Eric Eve aptly notes, "That a *human* agent should *heal* from a distance is remarkable; but praying for someone's healing from a distance is surely commonplace."[53]

---

53. Eve, *Jewish Context*, 289 (italics original).

# 4

# "Do You See This Woman?"

## Text

36 One of the Pharisees asked Jesus to eat with him, and he went into the Pharisee's house and took his place at the table. 37 And a woman in the city, who was a sinner, having learned that he was eating in the Pharisee's house, brought an alabaster jar of ointment. 38 She stood behind him at his feet, weeping, and began to bathe his feet with her tears and to dry them with her hair. Then she continued kissing his feet and anointing them with the ointment. 39 Now when the Pharisee who had invited him saw it, he said to himself, "If this man were a prophet, he would have known who and what kind of woman this is who is touching him—that she is a sinner." 40 Jesus spoke up and said to him, "Simon, I have something to say to you." "Teacher," he replied, "speak." 41 "A certain creditor had two debtors; one owed five hundred denarii, and the other fifty. 42 When they could not pay, he canceled the debts for both of them. Now which of them will love him more?" 43 Simon answered, "I suppose the one for whom he canceled the greater debt." And Jesus said to him, "You have judged rightly." 44 Then turning toward the woman, he said to Simon, "Do you see this woman? I entered your house; you gave me no water for my feet, but she has bathed my feet with her tears and dried them with her hair. 45 You gave me no kiss, but from the time I came in she has not stopped kissing my feet. 46 You did not anoint my head with oil, but she has anointed my feet with ointment. 47 Therefore, I tell you, her sins, which were many, have been forgiven; hence she has shown great love. But the one to whom little is forgiven, loves little." 48 Then he said to her, "Your sins are forgiven." 49 But

those who were at the table with him began to say among themselves, "Who is this who even forgives sins?" 50 And he said to the woman, "Your faith has saved you; go in peace."

Luke 7:36–50 (NRSV)[1]
(See also Matt 26:6–13; Mark 14:3–9; John 12:1–8)

## Scholarly Context

IN HIS PROLOGUE TO the Gospel, Luke informs Theophilus, his literary patron, that the orderly account of his written Gospel narrative is dependent on carefully investigating trustworthy oral and written sources related to the historical events surrounding Jesus' life, ministry, death, and resurrection (Luke 1:1–14). As already mentioned in chapters 1 and 3, Mark's Gospel and "Q" were definitely among the primary written sources Luke (and Matthew) utilized in writing his Gospel narrative about Jesus. Burnett Hillman Streeter proposed two additional sources for the material unique to Luke and Matthew, thus expanding the Two-Document Hypothesis into a Four-Document Hypothesis.[2] These additional non-Markan, non-"Q" sources, which are conveniently designated as "L" for Luke and "M" for Matthew, exclusively refer to peculiar material found only either in Luke's Gospel (e.g., Luke 1:5–25, 57–66; 7:11–17; 10:25–37; 15:11–32; 16:19–31; 18:9–14; 24:13–35) or Matthew's Gospel (e.g., Matt 1:18–25; 2:1–12; 14:28–31; 17:24–27; 25:31–46; 27:3–10). The material which occurs only in one Gospel belongs to the Single Tradition.[3] The vast majority of scholars put the date of the composition of Luke's Gospel between 80–85 CE.

The pericope of the sinful woman who comes to Jesus while he is dining at the house of Simon the Pharisee, wets his feet with her tears, dries them with her loosened hair, kisses them, and anoints them with aromatic ointment (Luke 7:36–50) is, in its actual state, substantially derived from Luke's special source material "L." Luke, in fact, is the only evangelist who preserves this distinctive and vivid tale of the triangular relationship between the woman's egregious breach of sociocultural etiquette, Simon the Pharisee's rejection of Jesus' prophetic status, and Jesus' confirmation and pronouncement of divine forgiveness of the many sins of the woman.

---

1. The pericope of Luke 7:36–50, or Luke 7:36—8:3, is liturgically read on the eleventh Sunday of Ordinary Time, Cycle C.

2. See further Streeter, *Four Gospels*, 223–70.

3. See Burridge, *Four Gospels?*, 11–12.

Luke's pericope, however, raises a host of important questions, most of which revolve around its relationship to the other three accounts of Jesus' anointing recorded in Matt 26:6–13, Mark 14:3–9, and John 12:1–8. The similarities and differences between them have been the subject of scholarly investigation.[4] It is clear that among the four accounts of Jesus' anointing are a number of striking similarities: (1) Jesus is a guest at a house; (2) he is reclining at table for a meal; (3) he is anointed by a woman with expensive aromatic ointment (μύρον, *myron*); (4) the woman's action triggers disapproval from a diner; and (5) Jesus comes to the immediate defense of the voiceless woman. Is this a coincidence? The situation becomes even more complicated when one considers that some other Lukan details share remarkable parallels with Matthew and Mark: (1) the host is named Simon (Luke 7:40; Matt 26:6; Mark 14:3); (2) the woman is anonymous and, apparently, an uninvited intruder (she is identified as Mary, the sister of Martha and Lazarus in John 11:2; 12:3); and (3) the aromatic ointment is carried in and poured from an alabaster jar (Luke 7:37; Matt 26:7; Mark 14:3). Furthermore, one is struck by the strong affinity between Luke and John. They both actually (1) use the same verb to describe the act of anointing (ἀλείφειν, *aleiphein*, "to anoint," Luke 7:38, 46; John 11:2; 12:3[5]), (2) assert that Jesus' feet are anointed, rather than his head as in Matthew 26:7 and Mark 14:3, and (3) state that Jesus' feet are wiped with hair (Luke 7:38; John 11:2; 12:3).

Nevertheless, many significant differences in locale, timing, theme, and peculiarities exist between Luke and the other three Gospel accounts of Jesus' anointing. First, Luke locates the pericope somewhere in Galilee, perhaps in or near the village of Nain (Luke 7:11), not in the village of Bethany on the eastern slope of the Mount of Olives in Judea, less than two miles away from Jerusalem, as in Matthew 26:6, Mark 14:3, and John 12:1. Second, and in connection with the previous point, Luke's pericope takes place earlier during Jesus' public ministry in Galilee, whereas the evangelists Matthew, Mark, and John agree on timing theirs shortly before Jesus' passion and crucifixion. Third, Luke's pericope associates the

---

4. See the discussion in Legault, "Application of the Form-Critique Method," 131–45; Dodd, *Historical Tradition*, 162–73; Elliott, "Anointing of Jesus," 105–7; Holst, "One Anointing," 435–46; Fitzmyer, *Gospel According to Luke I–IX*, 684–85; Coakley, "Anointing at Bethany," 241–56; Johnson, *Gospel of Luke*, 128–29; Bock, *Luke 1:1—9:50*, 1:689–91; Varghese, *Imagery of Love*, 171–75; Calduch-Benages, *Perfume of the Gospel*, 49–50; Mullen, *Dining with Pharisees*, 84–87.

5. See *BDAG*, 41.

fourfold action of the sinful woman with the themes of divine forgiveness and grateful love (Luke 7:41–47), while the evangelists Matthew, Mark, and John explicitly connect it to Jesus' impending death and burial (Matt 26:12; Mark 14:8; John 12:7). Fourth, some Lukan peculiarities are most distinctly conspicuous. Of the four evangelists, only Luke (1) designates the host as Simon the Pharisee (Luke 7:36 [twice], 37, 39), not Simon the leper (Matt 26:6; Mark 14:3; John does not specify who the host is [Lazarus?]), (2) identifies the anonymous woman as a sinner (Luke 7:37), (3) refers to the woman's outburst of emotion, viz., her tears (Luke 7:38), (4) states that the woman kisses Jesus' feet, (5) mentions Jesus' parable of the creditor and the two remitted debtors (Luke 7:41–43), and (6) presents Jesus' words on forgiveness, love, faith, and peace (Luke 7:41–50).

How can both striking similarities and remarkable differences between these four accounts of Jesus' anointing be satisfactorily understood and explained? Scholars have postulated at least two quite different possibilities. C. H. Dodd hypothesizes that behind the different accounts of Jesus' anointing unmistakably lies the same historical incident with variations and cross-combinations of different features and details, arising naturally in the course of oral transmission. Each evangelist independently used a separate strand of tradition, and the strands overlapped, and made relatively minor editorial contributions to the account in the process of having it put into crystallized written form.[6] André Legault contrarily postulates that the different accounts of Jesus' anointing radically describe two distinct historical incidents with different objectives. The first incident occurred in Galilee where a penitent woman intruded upon the dinner gathering, wept over Jesus' feet, wetted them, dried them with her hair, and kissed them. This incident, which lacks the reference to an alabaster jar of ointment and the act of anointing, lies behind Luke 7:36–50. The second incident took place in Bethany of Judea where a woman (Mary?) anointed Jesus' head with ointment in the house of Simon the leper where the three siblings—Lazarus, Martha, and Mary—were present. This incident is the backbone of Matthew 26:6–13, Mark 14:3–9, and John 12:1–8. These two incidents were already circulating as oral tradition in the community before being put in writing. They were often conflated. Eventually,

---

6. See Dodd, *Historical Tradition*, 172; cf. Elliot, "Anointing of Jesus," 105; Holst, "One Anointing," 446; Fitzmyer, *Gospel According to Luke I–IX*, 686; Corley, *Private Women*, 122; Bovon, *Luke 1*, 291.

certain details were juggled back and forth from one incident to the other, and elements of each were preserved.[7]

It is obvious that both scholars noticeably have one thing in common, viz., admitting that conflation and overlapping of certain features and details occurred during the period of oral transmission. The question of whether or not there is one single incident or two cannot be answered, therefore, with absolute certainty. However, recognizing that Matthew 26:6–13, Mark 14:3–9, and John 12:1–8 describe the same historical incident occurring at Bethany, though with minor differences, it is entirely tenable to maintain that the incident in Luke 7:36–50 relates another independent account of a woman who lavishly attends to Jesus' body,[8] with some elements from the incident of the anointing at Bethany being conflated with it in the process of oral transmission. One of the most conspicuous elements of conflation would probably be the introduction of Simon's name.[9] It is a bit strange that none of the Pharisees who invite Jesus over to a meal (Luke 11:37–54; 14:1–24) are actually named except Simon (Luke 7:40). The Lukan reference to the penitent woman wiping Jesus' feet with her loosened hair and smearing them with aromatic ointment must have come from an independent, primitive, and original tradition.[10] In any event, Luke's pericope needs to be explored on its own terms to fully appreciate its captivating narrative of perception and redemption.

## Literary Genre and Structure

The literary form of the present Lukan pericope is a composite of a controversy story, sparked by the arrival and fourfold action of the sinful woman (Luke 7:36–40, 44–47), a narrative parable about a creditor who remits the

---

7. See Legault, "Application of the Form-Critique Method," 143–45; cf. Taylor, *Formation of the Gospel Tradition*, 154–55; Taylor, *Gospel According to St. Mark*, 530; Brown, *Gospel According to John (I–XII)*, 449–52; Schweizer, *Good News According to Mark*, 228; Marshall, *Gospel of Luke*, 306; Witherington, *Women in the Ministry of Jesus*, 54; Witherington, *Women and the Genesis of Christianity*, 108; Johnson, *Gospel of Luke*, 129; Stein, *Luke*, 235; Bock, *Luke 1:1—9:50*, 691; Reid, *Choosing the Better* Part?, 109; Kilgallen, "Forgiveness of Sins," 115; Hultgren, *Parables of Jesus*, 213.

8. See further Köstenberger, "Comparison of the Pericopae," 49–63.

9. See Brown, *Gospel According to John (I–XII)*, 451; Hultgren, *Jesus and His Adversaries*, 84–87.

10. See Holst, "One Anointing," 436–37; Witherington, *Women and the Genesis of Christianity*, 109; Mullen, *Dining with Pharisees*, 90; Thomas, *Jesus' Meals*, 199.

debts of two debtors (Luke 7:41–43), and an appendage reflecting Lukan compositional style (Luke 7:48–50).[11]

As a sub-category of Rudolf Bultmann's apophthegms, a controversy story has a basic literary form consisting of a threefold pattern characteristic of rabbinic discussion.[12] First, the starting point lies in some action or attitude: Jesus does not object to the woman physically touching his feet (Luke 7:37–38). Second, the opponent seizes the action and uses it to stage an attack by accusation or question: Simon indignantly and silently objects that Jesus cannot be a prophet since he shows no knowledge that the woman is actually a sinner (Luke 7:39). Third, the dominical reply to the attack, which is brief and compact, comes at the end: Jesus' reply to Simon's criticism is given in the form of a parable about a creditor who remits the debts of two debtors and its subsequent application to Simon the Pharisee as well as the woman (Luke 7:41–47). Both the controversy story and the parable complete, complement, affect, and stand in tension with each other. It is now widely accepted that they formed from the start one composite narrative in the pre-Lukan source.[13] One should keep in mind that parables in Luke's Gospel are usually provided with narrative setting to function as a framework for interpreting them. Luke 10:25–37, which is an apophthegm framing the parable of the good Samaritan, is another good example.

In terms of structure, the pericope is carefully constructed. It unfolds in a very interesting way in five scenes: (1) introduction and description (Luke 7:36), (2) arrival and fourfold action of the sinful woman (Luke 7:37–38), (3) Simon's internal criticism of Jesus (Luke 7:39), (4) Jesus' riposte to Simon (Luke 7:40–47), and (5) Jesus' confirmation and pronouncement of forgiveness (Luke 7:48–50).

---

11. See Bultmann, *History of the Synoptic Tradition*, 20–21; Schweizer, *Good News According to Luke*, 137–138; Fitzmyer, *Gospel According to Luke I–IX*, 684–685; Hultgren, *Jesus and His Adversaries*, 86.

12. See Bultmann, *History of the Synoptic Tradition*, 39–45.

13. See Fitzmyer, *Gospel According to Luke I–IX*, 685; Marshall, *Gospel of Luke*, 305–7; Hultgren, *Parables of Jesus*, 215; Thomas, *Jesus' Meals*, 168; Ellis, *Gospel of Luke*, 121; Paffenroth, *Story of Jesus*, 35–36.

## Narrative Analysis

### Introduction and Description (Luke 7:36)

Regardless of the transmission history of the pericope, the opening verse of Luke 7:36 quickly sets the stage by introducing the characters and the setting with a minimum of exposition. In a startling move, τις . . . τῶν Φαρισαίων (*tis . . . tōn Pharisaiōn*, "a certain one . . . of the Pharisees") invites αὐτὸν (*auton*, "him") to come to his house for dinner (Luke 7:36). Note that the opening verse in Greek actually neither mentions the name of the host nor the name of the guest. Only later does Luke positively identify them as Simon and Jesus, respectively (Luke 7:40). Another noteworthy fact is that there is no indication within the pericope itself about the geographical location of the Pharisee's house. One is led, however, to the conclusion that its locale would probably have been at Nain, which Luke labels as πόλις (*polis*, "city," "town," Luke 7:11). Nain, mentioned only here in the entire Bible, is identified with the present-day Arabic village Nein, lying about five miles southeast of Nazareth, and probably meaning "pleasant" in Hebrew.[14]

Nothing more is said of the host other than being a Pharisee (Luke 7:36 [twice], 37, 39). The very word "Pharisee" seems to originate from an Aramaic root word פָּרַשׁ (*pāraš*), meaning "to separate oneself"[15]; hence, the Pharisees were the ones who kept themselves apart from anyone or anything that might have rendered them ritually impure. For example, they looked down upon עַם הָאָרֶץ (*'am hā 'ārês*, "people of the earth," "commoners," 2 Kgs 25:19; Jer 52:25[16]) and criticized them for their laxity in the personal observance of customs designed to maintain the Levitical code of ritual purity.[17]

As a prominent and influential religiopolitical force within Palestinian Judaism, the Pharisees likely emerged from the turmoil following the Maccabean revolt in 167–160 BCE against the Seleucid ruler, Antiochus IV Epiphanes, whose totalitarian policy attempted to enforce Hellenism by outlawing Jewish practices, such as circumcision, Sabbath observance, and dietary restrictions (1 Macc 1:41–50; 2 Macc 6:1; *J.W.* 1.1.2 §§34–35; *Ant.*

---

14. See Rousseau and Arav, *Jesus and His World*, 213.

15. See *BDB*, 831.

16. See *BDB*, 766–67.

17. See Jeremias, *Jerusalem in the Time of Jesus*, 259; Lachs, "Studies in the Semitic Background," 205; Boadt, *Reading the Old Testament*, 523; Vermes, *Complete Dead Sea Scrolls in English*, 117.

12.5.4 §§248–56).[18] It is a well-known fact that the Pharisees were largely lay teachers and experts who advocated strict interpretation and observance of the Mosaic law, and developed various oral traditions, acting as fences around the Torah (*J.W.* 2.8.14 §162; *Ant.* 13.10.6 §297; 17.2.4 §41). Some of the Pharisees' most distinctive theological views were the beliefs in the immortality and incorruptibility of human souls (*J.W.* 2.8.14 §163; *Ant.* 18.1.3 §14), the resurrection of the dead (Acts 23:6), and the existence of angels and spirits (Acts 23:8).[19] Just before the death of King Herod the Great, who ruled Judea between 37–4 BCE, there were more than 6,000 Pharisees who refused to take an oath of allegiance to both Caesar Augustus (27 BCE—14 CE) and Herod himself (*Ant.* 17.2.4 §42). Some Pharisees are mentioned by name in the New Testament, such as Nicodemus (John 3:1), Saul of Tarsus, known also as Paul (Acts 23:6; Phil 3:5), and Gamaliel (Acts 5:34; 22:23).

The invitation from the Pharisee, being the first of three accounts of Pharisaic banquets (Luke 7:36–50; 11:37–54; 14:1–24), is categorically unprecedented because, up to this point, the evangelist has already narrated some incidents (Luke 5:17–26, 27–32; 6:1–5) in which there is a mounting criticism leveled by members of the Pharisaic party against Jesus and his disciples (Luke 5:21, 30; 6:2). Moreover, when Jesus heals a man with a withered right hand on the Sabbath (Luke 6:6–10), the Pharisees are filled with mindless rage and discuss what to do with him (Luke 6:11). According to the evangelist, the Pharisees' rejection of the ministries of John the Baptist and Jesus is a rejection of God's plan (Luke 7:29–35). Why then does this particular Pharisee extend a dinner invitation to Jesus? The answer evidently lies in Jesus' charismatic fame. Upon witnessing Jesus' raising the widow's son from the dead at Nain (Luke 7:11–17), the crowd proclaims Jesus as a great prophet in their midst; and, consequently, the news about his prophetic ministry spreads throughout the region. This particular Pharisee must have heard this news (Luke 7:39). His invitation, therefore, shows that he is receptive and willing to find out the truth for himself about Jesus' prophetic credentials. There is no reason to believe that there are any sinister motives and nefarious objectives behind the invitation.[20]

Jesus accepts the Pharisee's invitation to dinner without any hesitation, as he has also accepted earlier the invitation to a great banquet in the

18. See also Sanders, *Historical Figure of Jesus*, 16–17.

19. See further Sanders, *Judaism*, 597–708.

20. See Plummer, *Critical and Exegetical Commentary*, 210; Fitzmyer, *Gospel According to Luke I–IX*, 688; Tannehill, *Luke*, 135; Green, *Gospel of Luke*, 307–8.

house of a toll collector named Levi (Luke 5:27–32). He goes into the Pharisee's house and reclines at the table. The verb κατακλίνειν (*kataklinein*, "to recline at dinner"[21]) is uniquely Lukan (Luke 7:36; 9:14–15; 14:8; 24:30). It gives the impression that the dinner is a formal and festive banquet, modeled along the lines of the Greco-Roman symposia genre,[22] where food and wine were served, discussions were held, social interactions took place, and entertainments were provided (Esth 1:5–9; Dan 5:1–4; Sir 31:12—32:13; 1 Macc 16:15). The customary posture for reclining required all male participants to remove sandals from their feet in order to be washed and dried. They then reclined on couches covered with pillows, rather than sitting on them. They leaned on their left elbows, facing a low common table at the center, with their feet stretched out away from the table. They used their right hands to eat and drink. The host arranged seating places for his guests according to their social rank and status.[23]

### *Arrival and Fourfold Action of the Sinful Woman (Luke 7:37–38)*

The Lukan phrase, καὶ ἰδού (*kai idou*, "and behold," "and look," Luke 7:37), which is employed some twenty-five times in this Gospel (e.g., Luke 1:20; 2:25; 5:12; 7:12; 8:41; 9:30; 10:25; 11:31; 13:11; 14:2; 19:2; 23:15; 24:4), draws attention to an important shift in the development of the narrative plot. The evangelist quickly introduces a new character and focuses the spotlight on her: γυνὴ ἥτις ἦν ἐν τῇ πόλει ἁμαρτωλός (*gynē hētis ēn en tē polei hamartōlos*, "a woman who was in the city a sinner," Luke 7:37). Note that this female minor character is anonymous, and her only identifying characteristic is that she is labeled as ἁμαρτωλός (*hamartōlos*, "sinner," "sinful"[24]). What exactly does this term mean? Does it insinuate that she was a gentile? A non-Jew? Jews labeled gentiles "sinners," probably because they did not have the Mosaic law (Gal 2:15). Does it suggest that she was involved in a degrading and repugnant occupation known for its dishonesty or immorality?[25] Does it imply that she was one of the רְשָׁעִים (*rĕšāʿîm*, "wicked ones"[26]), who

---

21. See *BDAG*, 518.

22. See Steele, "Luke 11:37–54," 380–87.

23. See Smith, *From Symposium to Eucharist*, 25–26; Bock, *Luke 1:1—9:50*, 694; Green, *Gospel of Luke*, 306; Tannehill, *Luke*, 135.

24. See *BDAG*, 51–52.

25. See further Jeremias, *Jerusalem in the Time of Jesus*, 303–12.

26. See *BDB*, 957.

heinously and willfully disobeyed the law and renounced the covenant?[27] Does it indicate that her socioreligious conduct disregarded matters of ritual purity and opposed the sectarian mentality and interpretation of the law?[28] It is obvious that there seems to be a lack of scholarly consensus regarding the identity of the "sinner" in Luke's Gospel.[29]

What makes this woman a sinner is unspecified by Luke. It is remarkable, however, how many scholars are too quick to jump to a conclusion that characterizes the nature of her sinfulness as the sin of prostitution,[30] "as if that is the only sin a woman is capable of committing."[31] This conclusion, at best, relies largely upon circumstantial evidence. It has been often suggested that (1) the expression, ἐν τῇ πόλει ἁμαρτωλός (*en tē polei hamartōlos,* "in the city a sinner"), is a clear euphemistic reference to a city prostitute known to the public; (2) the woman's audacious intrusion on an all-male formal banquet symposium affair is scandalous; and (3) the woman's fourfold action toward Jesus constitutes a serious breach of sociocultural decorum of first-century Palestinian Judaism.[32] That the anonymous woman is not a notorious city prostitute is obvious because the term ἁμαρτωλός (*hamartolos*), which is used about eighteen times in this Gospel (Luke 5:8, 30, 32; 6:32, 33, 34 [twice]; 7:34, 37, 39; 13:2; 15:1, 2, 7, 10; 18:13; 19:7; 24:7) never refers to prostitution. Both Barbara E. Reid and Teresa J. Hornsby correctly comment that no scholar would read Simon Peter's self-identification and self-characterization as a "sinful man" in Luke 5:8 and draw an inference that Simon Peter's sinfulness was actually about sexual immorality and deviancy.[33] There is also no textual basis for the identification of the woman in Luke 7:36–50 with Mary Magdalene (Luke 8:2), Mary of Bethany (Luke 10:38–42; John 11:1), or even the anonymous adulteress (John 7:53—8:11).[34]

---

27. See further Sanders, *Jesus and Judaism,* 174–211.

28. See further Dunn, *Jesus, Paul, and the Law,* 73–77.

29. See further Adams, *Sinner in Luke,* ix–xviii.

30. See Plummer, *Critical and Exegetical Commentary,* 210; Schweizer, *Good News According to Luke,* 139; Green, *Gospel of Luke,* 309; Bock, *Luke 1:1—9:50,* 695; Bovon, *Luke 1,* 293; Witherington, *Women in the Ministry of Jesus,* 54; Marshall, *Gospel of Luke,* 308; Stein, *Luke,* 236; Ellis, *Gospel of Luke,* 122; Barclay, *Gospel of Luke,* 113.

31. Levine and Witherington, *Gospel of Luke,* 210.

32. See Corley, *Private Women,* 124–25; Applegate, "'Ands She Wets His Feet with Her Tears,'" 78–79.

33. See Reid, *Choosing the Better Part?,* 115; Hornsby, "Why Is She Crying?", 93.

34. In F. Zeffirelli's 1977 six-hour television mini-series *Jesus of Nazareth,* the woman

Having known that Jesus is reclining at a dinner banquet at the Pharisee's house, the sinful woman brings with her ἀλάβαστρον μύρου (*alabastron myrou*, "an alabaster flask of aromatic ointment," Luke 7:37), containing precious and perfumed ointment made of olive oil infused with various spices (Exod 30:23–25). The alabaster jar would have been tightly sealed at the neck to best keep the aromatic scent of the ointment pure and unspoiled (*Nat.* 13.3 §19). The sinful woman ventures into the all-male banquet room, in all probability, stealthily. Her move is undeniably audacious, revealing her determination to reach Jesus, who is reputed to be a φίλος (*philos*, "friend," Luke 7:34[35]) of sinners. She manages to position herself behind τοὺς πόδας αὐτοῦ (*tous podas autou*, "his feet"), a phrase appearing three times in Luke 7:38. As she struggles to regain her composure, tears fall profusely from her eyes, like a dam that has just burst. Bowing down, she moistens his feet with her tears, wipes them with the unbound hairs of her head, kisses his feet, and finally smears them with the aromatic ointment of her alabaster jar. Although she does not utter a single word, her fourfold action, which overrides all sociocultural norms and codes of etiquettes, speaks louder than words.

What is one, however, to make of this scene? Some scholars construe the woman's lavish treatment of Jesus as conveying sensual nuances, erotic overtones, or sexual innuendos.[36] Such a notion is very far-fetched because, unlike a morally lax Greco-Roman symposium, (1) the Pharisaic host does not supply the woman to sexually fondle Jesus' feet; (2) the setting of the Lukan banquet is in a room at the Galilean house of the Pharisee, who is known to be a zealous adherent to daily ritual purity; (3) the woman is shedding tears, which are a caution for any sensual, erotic, or sexual interpretation of Luke 7:38; and (4) the woman's fourfold action expresses deep reverence and profound gratitude, confidence, and service for Jesus (cf. Luke

---

in Luke 7:36–50 is, unfortunately, (1) called a whore, (2) identified with Mary Magdalene, (3) confused with the anonymous adulteress in John 7:53—8:11 (R. Powell, playing Jesus, says to A. Bancroft, playing the sinful woman/Mary Magdalene: "Go, sin no more," cf. John 8:11), and (4) spoken to as Mary of Bethany in John 12:1–8 (R. Powell, playing Jesus, says to A. Bancroft, playing the sinful woman/Mary Magdalene: "Take this ointment and keep it for my burial," cf. John 12:7). This uncogent amalgamation of these four different women into one female persona is reminiscent of the writing of St. Ephraim the Syrian (ca. 306–373 CE) and the homily of Pope Gregory the Great (540–604 CE).

35. See *BDAG*, 1058–59.

36. See, for instance, Schweizer, *Good News According to Luke*, 139; Corley, *Private Women*, 125; Green, *Gospel of Luke*, 310; Mullen, *Dining with Pharisees*, 111.

8:35, 41; 10:39; 17:16).[37] It must, of course, be admitted that the fourfold action of the sinful woman was indecorous because it violated normative Jewish patriarchal culture and the sensibilities of that time. For example, it was widely considered very shameful for a woman to uncover her head and let her hair down in public (cf. 1 Cor 11:5–6). Any woman who behaved in such a manner was regarded to have loose morals (*b. Yoma* 47a). Nevertheless, the sinful woman makes an audacious move and uses the only viable means—her hair—as a substitution for a towel to dry Jesus' feet before kissing and anointing them with aromatic ointment.

The evangelist does not furnish any information whatsoever about why the sinful woman has come to Jesus and what kind of overwhelming emotion has brought her to tears. There are two scenarios to consider.[38] She comes to Jesus, seeking divine forgiveness of him. Her loving, fourfold action is penitential, expressing the condition of her remorseful and sorrowful heart over the sinful life she has led. Therefore, in this first scenario, her loving, fourfold action elicits and leads to divine forgiveness and peace (Luke 7:47a, 48, 50).[39] Contrarily, the no-longer sinful woman comes to Jesus, seeking to express her grateful love for the divine forgiveness she has already received for her many sins during a previous encounter with Jesus. The reality of such an earlier encounter, viz., the when and how the sinful woman has experienced forgiveness, is unnarrated by Luke. It can only be presumed. Thus, in this second scenario, her loving, fourfold action is a response to, and demonstration of, her prior divine forgiveness (Luke 7:41–43, 47b).[40] Ultimately, it all depends on one's reading of the enigmatic and notorious verse of Luke 7:47.

---

37. See Cosgrove, "Woman's Unbound Hair," 688; Fitzmyer, *Gospel According to Luke I–IX*, 689; Edwards, *Gospel According to Luke*, 226–28; Bock, *Luke 1:1—9:50*, 697; Calduch-Benages, *Perfume of the Gospel*, 58.

38. See Fitzmyer, *Gospel According to Luke I–IX*, 686–87; Kilgallen, "Forgiveness of Sins," 105; Hägerland, *Jesus and the Forgiveness of Sins*, 52–53.

39. See, for example, Applegate, "'Ands She Wets His Feet with Her Tears,'" 76; Jipp, *Divine Visitations*, 181.

40. Most scholars are of the opinion that the woman comes to Jesus already forgiven prior to the pericope of Luke 7:36–50. See, for example, Plummer, *Critical and Exegetical Commentary*, 214; Fitzmyer, *Gospel According to Luke I–IX*, 687; Tannehill, *Luke*, 135; Green, *Gospel of Luke*, 308; Bock, *Luke 1:1—9:50*, 695; Carroll, *Luke*, 177; Edwards, *Gospel According to Luke*, 230–31; Levine and Witherington, *Gospel of Luke*, 211; Corley, *Private Women*, 125; Marshall, *Gospel of Luke*, 306; Stein, *Luke*, 237–38; Kilgallen, "Proposal for Interpreting Luke 7,36–50," 327; Kilgallen, "Faith and Forgiveness," 383.

## Simon's Internal Criticism of Jesus (Luke 7:39)

Through a narrative aside, the evangelist shifts the focus of attention from the ministrations of the woman to the host of the banquet. Unlike Jesus, who silently accepts the woman's fourfold action without judgment, the Pharisee studiously watches the strange, real-life spectacle unfolding before his eyes. He, consequently, engages in a captious internal monologue (εἶπεν ἐν ἑαυτῷ, *eipen en heautō*, "he spoke within himself," "he said to himself," Luke 7:39; cf. Luke 7:49; 16:3; 18:4), which reveals the deepest thought of his heart. Notice how Simon thinks of Jesus: Οὗτος εἰ ἦν προφήτης, ἐγίνωσκεν ἂν τίς καὶ ποταπὴ ἡ γυνὴ ἥτις ἅπτεται αὐτοῦ, ὅτι ἁμαρτωλός ἐστιν (*Houtos ei ēn prophētēs, eginōsken an tis kai potapē hē gynē hētis haptetai autou, hoti hamartōlos estin*, "If this [man] was [were] a prophet, he would know who and what woman [is this] who touches him, for she is a sinner," Luke 7:39).

Three things can irrefutably be extrapolated from the host's soliloquy. First, the host's reference to Jesus as Οὗτος (*Houtos*, "this [man]") has a contemptuous undertone. Second, the host's contrary-to-fact conditional statement, "If this [man] was [were] a prophet, he would know who and what woman [is this] who touches him, for she is a sinner," is erroneous because at its core lies an assumption that Jesus is not a prophet (of course, he is), and a conclusion that Jesus lacks the power of clairvoyance, for he obviously does not know the character of the woman (of course, he does). The Pharisee, therefore, has already failed in his interpretation of Jesus' prophetic stature. Third, the host's counterfactual thought aims at maintaining a stark distance and separation between himself, on the one hand, and Jesus and the sinful woman, on the other hand. One cannot help but think that the host must have felt utterly disappointed and bitterly regretful for inviting Jesus at all.

## Jesus' Riposte to Simon (Luke 7:40–47)

Becoming cognizant of the interior thought of the Pharisaic host, Jesus takes the initiative to openly engage him in a dialectical conversation, politely addressing him by his first name and respectfully requesting permission to speak, Σίμων, ἔχω σοί τι εἰπεῖν (*Simōn, echō soi ti eipein*, "Simon, I have something to say to you," Luke 7:40). In Luke's Gospel, Jesus, as God's final, supreme agent in the history of salvation, demonstrates his prophetic stature in his ability to know, perceive, read, and answer the inner dispositions of others (e.g., Luke 5:21–22; 6:7–8; 9:46–47; 11:15–17, 37–39; 20:21–26; 24:37–38). Coldly, Simon responds to his guest of honor with a short reply, Διδάσκαλε, εἰπέ (Didaskale, eipe, "Teacher, speak," Luke 7:40). The title διδάσκαλος (didaskalos, "teacher"[41]) appears seventeen times in this Gospel (Luke 2:46; 3:12; 6:40 [twice]; 7:40; 8:49; 9:38; 10:25; 11:45; 12:13; 18:18; 19:39; 20:21, 28, 39; 21:7; 22:11). It is used in reference to the Jewish teachers in the Jerusalem Temple (Luke 2:46), John the Baptist (Luke 3:12), and Jesus (Luke 7:40; 8:49; 9:38; 10:25; 11:45; 12:13; 18:18; 19:39; 20:21, 28, 39; 21:7; 22:11). It is the Greek translation of the Aramaic רַבִּי (rabbî, "my lord/Lord," "my master," "my teacher," cf. John 1:38). It was a common and formal title, signifying honor, dignity, and respect. However, as the context of Luke 7:39 shows, Simon's address to Jesus as διδάσκαλος (didaskalos) does not necessarily indicate a positive response to Jesus.[42]

Instead of replying with a string of rebukes, Jesus then proceeds to tell his host a straightforward parable of a creditor who graciously remits substantial amounts of outstanding debts of two debtors—an act unparalleled and unheard of—because they lack adequate funds to repay their debts (cf. Matt 18:21–35). One client is involved in a debt of 500 denarii, and the other owes a debt of fifty denarii. A δηνάριον (dēnarion, Luke 7:41[43]), a Roman silver coin, was the usual daily wage for a laborer and soldier (Matt 20:2; Ann. 1:17). Interestingly, the verb χαρίζεσθαί (charizesthai, "to cancel a sum of money that is owed," Luke 7:41[44]) conveys the nuance of granting forgiveness (cf. 2 Cor 2:5–11; Col 3:13). In this sense, the creditor freely and graciously forgives the entire debts of both debtors. Significantly, the word "debt" is used as a metaphor for "sin."[45] Nowhere is this substitution more evident than in the Lord's Prayer (Matt 6:9–13; Luke 11:2–4). In terms of noun usage, Matthew uses ὀφείλημα (opheilēma, "debt," as in "and forgive us our debts," Matt 6:12[46]), while Luke employs ἁμαρτία (hamartia, "sin," as in "and forgive us our sins," Luke 11:4[47]). Underlying both of these Greek

---

41. See BDAG, 241.
42. See Johnson, Gospel of Luke, 127.
43. See BDAG, 223.
44. See BDAG, 1078.
45. See McNamara, Targum and Testament Revisited, 187; Anderson, Sin, 27.
46. See BDAG, 743.
47. See BDAG, 50–51.

interchangeable words is Jesus' original Aramaic word חוֹבָא (*ḥôbā*[48]). Whoever sins becomes indebted to God.

Jesus ends the parable with a direct question for Simon to ponder: τίς οὖν αὐτῶν πλεῖον ἀγαπήσει αὐτόν (*tis oun autōn pleion agapēsei auton*, "Which of them therefore will love him more?," Luke 7:42). Pushed into a corner, the host answers without hesitation or reluctance, "I assume that to whom he remitted the most" (Luke 7:43). His cautiously formulated verdict wins the approval of Jesus, Ὀρθῶς ἔκρινας (*Orthōs ekrinas*, "Correctly you judged," Luke 7:43). At this juncture, it is important to highlight certain incontrovertible premises underlying Jesus' parable (Luke 7:41–43). First, the larger the remission of the debt, the greater the love is produced in the debtor. Second, there is an inextricable correlation between remission of the debt and forgiveness of the sin. Third, the parable has a certain allegorical character.[49] The creditor is a metaphor for God, the two debtors depict Simon (characterized as the lesser debtor) and the woman (identified with the greater debtor), the debt represents sin, and the remission of the debt indicates the forgiveness of sin. Luke 7:44–47, where Jesus applies the parable to Simon and the woman, will prove these premises to be true.

Facing now the woman while still talking to Simon, Jesus' deliberate body language functions as an implicit rebuke to the host. His question, Βλέπεις ταύτην τὴν γυναῖκα (*Blepeis tautēn tēn gynaika*, "Do you see this woman?," Luke 7:44), is an explicit invitation to the Pharisee to see the female intruder in a new and different light, through the parable, not as a sinner, but as an already-forgiven woman whose fourfold action is an expression of grateful love. The verb βλέπειν (*blepein*[50]) is not only used in reference to the physical act of seeing with eyes (e.g., Luke 7:21; 8:16), but also applied figuratively to one's mental perception of reality (e.g., Luke 8:10; 10:24).

To help the host understand what is at stake here, Jesus makes a stark and threefold contrasting statement between the Pharisee's behavior and that of the woman. The adversative δὲ (*de*, "but," Luke 7:44, 45, 46) serves to contrast two differing responses to Jesus in each statement, viz., the inhospitality of Simon the Pharisee and the hospitality of the woman. First, Simon does not provide Jesus with water and towels to wash and dry his dusty feet,

---

48. See *BDB*, 295.

49. See Fitzmyer, *Gospel According to Luke I–IX*, 687; Hultgren, *Parables of Jesus*, 214–15.

50. See *BDAG*, 178–79.

but the woman moistens Jesus' feet with her tears and wipes them with her hair (Luke 7:44). The custom of washing a guest's feet on entering a house was regarded as a sign of hospitality (Gen 18:4; 19:2; 24:32; 43:24; Judg 19:21; 1 Sam 25:41; John 13:5; 1 Tim 5:10). Second, Simon does not greet Jesus with a kiss on the cheek upon his arrival to the house, but the woman keeps kissing Jesus' feet (Luke 7:45). Customarily, the kiss of greeting was a common ancient practice to show cordiality and respect (Gen 29:13; 33:4; Exod 18:7; 2 Sam 15:5; Luke 15:20; 22:47-48; 1 Thess 5:26; 1 Cor 16:20; Rom 16:16). Third, Simon does not anoint Jesus' head with ἔλαιον (elaion, "olive oil"[51]), a cheap, common, and everyday oil, but the woman smears Jesus' feet with an expensive aromatic ointment (Luke 7:46). While anointing a guest's head with olive oil displays a mark of respect and warm hospitality (Pss 23:5; 133:2; Mark 14:3), rubbing a guest's feet with costly, perfumed oil shows utter devotion and service (Deut 33:24; Od. 19:503-7). The two obvious conclusions to be drawn from this juxtaposition are: (1) Jesus does not construe the woman's fourfold action, as narrated in Luke 7:38 and retold in Luke 7:44-46, in sensual, erotic, or sexual terms, but rather interprets it as a gesture of hospitality and complete self-devotion; and (2) Simon's failure to properly receive Jesus constitutes an infringement of the codes and laws of hospitality. "Simon's reception of Jesus," writes David B. Gowler, "is at best lukewarm and at worst shameful."[52]

Jesus concludes his rebuttal of the Pharisee with a climactic statement, bringing into sharp focus all pieces of the narrative, viz., Simon, the woman, and the parable. He directly says to his host, "This, therefore, I say to you, her many sins have been forgiven because she loved much; but to whom little is forgiven, loves little" (Luke 7:47). Bear in mind that this most straightforward translation is problematic. There is some tension, if not outright contradiction, between Luke 7:47a and Luke 7:47b. The first half of the sentence, "her many sins have been forgiven because she loved much" (Luke 7:47a) implies that the love of the woman is the cause and basis for divine forgiveness. However, this reading is immediately rectified by the second half, "but to whom little is forgiven, loves little" (Luke 7:47b), which emphatically states that love follows and flows out of forgiveness. In this case, the love of the woman is the consequence and evidence of divine forgiveness. To solve this dilemma, the conjunction ὅτι (hoti, "because," "for," Luke 7:47) in the ὅτι-clause (ὅτι ἠγάπησεν

---

51. See BDAG, 313.

52. Gowler, Host, Guest, Enemy and Friend, 225.

πολύ, *hoti ēgapēsen poly*, Luke 7:47a) is understood not in a causal sense ("*because* she loved much"), but in a logical sense ("*as is evidenced by the fact that* she loved much").[53] John T. Carroll writes that "the woman's actions, expressing love, are the reason Jesus can say that she has received forgiveness, not the reason she has been forgiven."[54] This interpretation agrees with the rationale of Jesus' parable, where the creditor's gracious remission of the debt leads to love (Luke 7:41–43). Furthermore, the verb ἀφιέναι (*aphienai*, "to cancel," "to remit," "to forgive"[55]) is used in the perfect passive tense (ἀφέωνται, *apheōntai*, "have been forgiven," Luke 7:47a), denoting an action completed in the past whose effects continue to the present. God, who is the direct agent of such action (Luke 5:20, 23), has already and graciously forgiven the woman all the sins she accumulated over the years prior to pouring out gestures of grateful love on Jesus. Simon, however, remains oblivious to the fact that the woman had undergone an existential metamorphosis. Jesus' remark to him that the woman's "many sins have been forgiven" (Luke 7:47) demonstrates that he is indeed a prophet who knows who the woman is. The woman has been in a state of forgiveness and newness. If this interpretation holds, then the imperfect verb ἦν (*ēn*, Luke 7:37) should not be translated as "was," as does NRSV ("a woman in the city who was a sinner," Luke 7:37), but rather as "used to be" ("a woman in the city who *used to be* a sinner"), because, according to Barbara E. Reid, "she is no longer the sinner she once was."[56]

### Jesus' Confirmation and Pronouncement of Forgiveness (Luke 7:48–50)

Jesus now turns to speak to the woman directly for the first time in the entire pericope, saying: "Your sins have been forgiven" (Luke 7:48). These words, simple and strong, function as a public theological confirmation and pronouncement of divine forgiveness, which has released the woman from the grip of sin. Concerned with the status, honor, and dignity of the woman, Jesus is still subtly and indirectly talking to Simon, inviting him to let go of his prejudiced treatment of the woman as an outcast (Luke 7:39)

---

53. See Plummer, *Critical and Exegetical Commentary*, 213; Moule, *Idiom Book*, 147; Fitzmyer, *Gospel According to Luke I–IX*, 692; Marshall, *Gospel of Luke*, 313; Stein, *Luke*, 237; Bovon, *Luke 1*, 297; Ellis, *Gospel of Luke*, 122.

54. Carroll, *Luke*, 180.

55. See BDAG, 156–57.

56. Reid, *Choosing the Better Part?*, 113.

and, consequently, play a crucial part in restoring the forgiven woman into the socioreligious life of the community.

Jesus' words trigger a complaint among other diners at the table, who appear to hold Pharisaic opinions (cf. Luke 5:21). Like the host, they too engage in an interior monologue, posing a question about Jesus' identity, Τίς οὗτός ἐστιν ὃς καὶ ἁμαρτίας ἀφίησιν (*Tis houtos estin hos kai hamartias aphiēsin*, "Who is this who even forgives sins?," Luke 7:49). To ask the question in this way would be to misunderstand and misconstrue Jesus' theological confirmation and pronouncement. Thus, instead of understanding that the merciful God is the source of the woman's forgiveness, the other guests perceive Jesus in their minds as claiming for himself the divine prerogative. As God's supreme agent of mercy, who has come to call sinners to μετάνοια (*metanoia*, "change of mind," "repentance," "conversion," Luke 5:32[57]), Jesus is commissioned to pronounce the divine gift of forgiveness (cf. Luke 5:24). Having ignored the question of the fellow diners, Jesus speaks to the woman directly for the second time, "Your faith has saved you" (Luke 7:50). Jesus' final words, which are almost identical to the formula used in Mark 5:34 (cf. Mark 10:52; Luke 8:48; 17:19), make clear that it is the faith of the woman that motivated her in the first place to seek God's forgiveness. Faith, in this context, is confidence and trust in God, whose forgiveness is always accessible and available. The scene comes to an end with Jesus' dismissal of the woman, "go into peace/go in peace" (Luke 7:50). All she needs to do is to live as one restored, forgiven, and redeemed. The evangelist, however, leaves the entire pericope open-ended as far as Simon the Pharisee is concerned.

57. See *BDAG*, 640–41.

# 5

# "He Received Him Rejoicing"

## Text

1 He entered Jericho and was passing through it. 2 A man was there named Zacchaeus; he was a chief toll collector and was rich. 3 He was trying to see who Jesus was, but on account of the crowd he could not, because he was short in stature. 4 So he ran ahead and climbed a sycamore tree to see him, because he was going to pass that way. 5 When Jesus came to the place, he looked up and said to him, "Zacchaeus, hurry and come down; for I must stay at your house today." 6 So he hurried down and was happy to welcome him. 7 All who saw it began to grumble and said, "He has gone to be the guest of one who is a sinner." 8 Zacchaeus stood there and said to the Lord, "Look, half of my possessions, Lord, I will give to the poor; and if I have defrauded anyone of anything, I will pay back four times as much." 9 Then Jesus said to him, "Today salvation has come to this house, because he too is a son of Abraham. 10 For the Son of Man came to seek out and to save the lost."

Luke 19:1–10 (NRSV)[1]

## Scholarly Context

THE PERICOPE OF ZACCHAEUS, a wealthy Jewish chief toll collector who offers hospitality to Jesus in the town of Jericho (Luke 19:1–10), is found only in Luke's Gospel. There is every reason to believe that this *Sondergut* pericope is indisputably taken from Luke's special source material "L." It is also possible that the pericope is directly traceable to an Aramaic source, which the evangelist himself may have translated into Greek. The frequent use of the paratactic conjunction (καὶ, *kai*, "and"), which appears fourteen

---

1. The pericope of Luke 19:1–10 is liturgically read on the thirty-first Sunday of Ordinary Time, Cycle C.

times in the pericope to connect short clauses, suggests an Aramaic pre-Lukan influence.[2] Nevertheless, the pericope, in its present form, bears the stamp of Lukan literary artistry, compositional activity, and theological ingenuity.[3] The evangelist has thoroughly edited it to thematically and climactically exemplify his theological understanding of the inclusive nature of salvation brought by Jesus' outreach to and association with the social, religious, and moral outcasts of first-century Palestinian society. As it stands, the pericope forms part of the lengthy structure of the central section of Luke's Gospel, often called the Travel Narrative, a *terminus technicus* among scholars to describe Luke's portrayal of Jesus' resolution to travel to Jerusalem (Luke 9:51—19:48).[4] Contextually, the location of the pericope is preponderant. The evangelist has purposefully and carefully inserted it into the framework of his Markan source by placing it immediately after the pericope of the healing of the blind man (Luke 18:35-43 || Mark 10:46-52) and shortly before Jesus' entry into Jerusalem (Luke 19:28-44 || Mark 11:1-11) to indicate its narrative importance as an epitome and a microcosm of the universality of salvation and redemption.

Situating the pericope within the context of the larger Lukan Gospel narrative irrefutably enhances its significance. It is quite obvious that the pericope combines and contains a cluster of prominent and recurring Lukan themes, such as: (1) depicting toll collectors as responding positively to the preaching of John the Baptist (Luke 3:12-13; 7:29) as well as to the ministry of Jesus (Luke 5:27-32; 15:1-2; 18:9-14; 19:1-10), so Zacchaeus, as a chief toll collector, seeks Jesus and welcomes him into his house with joy; (2) employing a reversal theme, as a literary device, to explicitly and implicitly overturn social values, expectations, and attitudes (Luke 1:51-53; 6:20-21, 24-25; 7:36-50; 10:25-37; 14:7-24; 15:3-32; 16:19-31; 18:15-17;

2. See Godet, *Commentary on the Gospel of St. Luke*, 417, 419; Plummer, *Critical and Exegetical Commentary*, 432; Knox, *Sources of the Synoptic Gospels*, 2:112; Schweizer, *Good News According to Luke*, 290; Fitzmyer, *Gospel According to Luke X–XXIV*, 1219; Marshall, *Gospel of Luke*, 695; Nolland, *Luke 18:35—24:43*, 903-4; Paffenroth, *Story of Jesus*, 64-65; Kinman, *Jesus' Entry into Jerusalem*, 80.

3. See further Loewe, "Towards an Interpretation," 321-31; O'Hanlon, "Story of Zacchaeus," 2-26.

4. See further Robinson, "Theological Context," 20-31; Gill, "Observations on the Lukan Travel Narrative," 199-221; Matera, "Jesus' Journey," 57-77; Bruehler, *Public and Political Christ*, 197-99. There is no scholarly consensus regarding the extent of the Lukan Travel Narrative. On this point, see further Ó Fearghail, *Introduction to Luke-Acts*, 48-51; Denaux, *Studies in the Gospel of Luke*, 3-32.

19:1–10),[5] thus Zacchaeus's characterization is reversed from a sinner to a changed and saved son of Abraham; and (3) inextricably connecting the (in)correct use of possessions with (lack of) salvation (Luke 3:11; 12:13–21; 14:33; 16:19–31; 18:18–30; 19:1–10; 21:1–4; Acts 2:42–47; 4:32–37; 5:1–11), hence Zacchaeus, who is said to be wealthy, receives salvation after publicly divulging his intention to generously give half of his possessions to the poor and compensate fourfold those he has defrauded. Furthermore, as will be later illustrated, the pericope has a number of significant linguistic similarities with and connections to other Lukan pericopae.

Despite the apparent simplicity of the pericope, the precise meaning and implication of Zacchaeus's declaration in Luke 19:8 has long been a *crux interpretum* since the publication of Frédéric L. Godet's commentary on Luke's Gospel in 1864–65. As a result, there has been considerable and ongoing debate among scholars as to how the two present indicative active verbs of διδόναι (*didonai*, "to give"[6]) and ἀποδιδόναι (*apodidonai*, "to give back"[7]) in Zacchaeus's declaration should be translated. Are these two verbs examples of the futuristic present ("I shall give [back]," "I am going to give [back]") or examples of the iterative or customary present ("I [customarily, regularly] give [back]")?[8] "The difference in interpretations," as Alan C. Mitchell rightly comments, "substantially affects the meaning of the pericope."[9] Currently, there are two opposing interpretations. The view of many, perhaps most, scholars is that the pericope is intrinsically a salvation story, depicting Zacchaeus's radical *metanoia*, which is initiated by his personal encounter with Jesus and substantiated through his voluntary acts of generosity and compensation. In this interpretation, Zacchaeus's declaration reveals his resolve and what he is about to do in the immediate future as a result of a changed heart. If so, "the lost," viz., Zacchaeus, has been sought and found. Scholars who support this interpretation translate the two present verbs as examples of the futuristic present.[10] Conversely, a relatively small

5. See further York, *Last Shall be First*, 39–163.

6. See *BDAG*, 242–43.

7. See *BDAG*, 109–10.

8. See Robertson, *Grammar of the Greek New Testament*, 869–70, 880.

9. Mitchell, "Zacchaeus Revisited," 153.

10. See, for instance, Plummer, *Critical and Exegetical Commentary*, 435; Schweizer, *Good News According to Luke*, 292; Marshall, *Gospel of Luke*, 697–98; Ireland, *Stewardship and the Kingdom of God*, 192; Nolland, *Luke 18:35—24:43*, 906–7; Bock, *Luke 9:51—24:53*, 1520; Tannehill, *Luke*, 277; Tannehill, *Shape of Luke's Story*, 76; Ellis, *Gospel of Luke*, 221; Edwards, *Gospel According to Luke*, 532; Stein, *Luke*, 466; Hamm, "Luke

number of scholars propound that the pericope is basically an *apologia* story, portraying Zacchaeus's vigorous defense to prove himself innocent against the unjust accusation leveled against him by his critics (Luke 19:7) by means of describing his customary conduct of generosity and compensation. In this interpretation, Zacchaeus's declaration discloses his defense of himself as a faithful Jew and what he has been habitually and regularly practicing all along. If so, "the lost," viz., Zacchaeus, has been exonerated and vindicated. Scholars who uphold this interpretation translate the two present verbs as examples of the iterative or customary present.[11]

## Literary Genre and Structure

There is some disagreement among scholars as to the precise literary genre of the pericope of Zacchaeus. A plethora of different and numerous classifications have been proposed, emphasizing different themes in the pericope. Martin Dibelius, with later endorsement from I. Howard Marshall, calls it a genuine personal legend, full of anecdotal peculiarities, such as the reference to Zacchaeus's name and small stature, which point to its historicity.[12] Rudolf Bultmann categorizes it as a biographical apophthegm, which is a brief unit, consisting of a concise, decisive, and independent saying of Jesus, appended to it to form a climactic conclusion. The dominical saying (Luke 19:[9]10), which is the main point of a biographical apophthegm, is called forth by Zacchaeus's conduct (Luke 19:8).[13] Vincent Taylor lists it as a story about Jesus, where interest appears to lie in the incident itself and its details rather than in Jesus' words, thus lacking a distinctive structural form.[14] Joseph A. Fitzmyer prefers to class it as a pronouncement story, with its climax in Luke 19:9.[15] Robert C. Tannehill, followed later by

---

19:8," 431–37; Hamm, "Zacchaeus Revisited," 249–52; O'Toole, "Literary Form of Luke 19:1–10," 108–9; Mendez-Moratalla, *Paradigm of Conversion in Luke*, 156; Adams, *Sinner in Luke*, 174; Bovon, *Luke 2*, 598–99; Harris, *Davidic Shepherd King*, 141–43.

11. See, for example, Godet, *Commentary on the Gospel of St. Luke*, 418; Fitzmyer, *Gospel According to Luke X–XXIV*, 1220–21; Green, *Gospel of Luke*, 671–72; White, "Vindication for Zacchaeus?," 21; Mitchell, "Zacchaeus Revisited," 153–76; Mitchell, "Use of συκοφαντεῖν," 546–47; Ravens, "Zacchaeus," 19–32; Johnson, *Gospel of Luke*, 285–86.

12. See Dibelius, *From Tradition to Gospel*, 50–51, 118; Marshall, *Gospel of Luke*, 695.

13. See Bultmann, *History of the Synoptic Tradition*, 11, 55–56, 61–63.

14. See Taylor, *Formation of the Gospel Tradition*, 75–76, 142.

15. See Fitzmyer, *Gospel According to Luke X–XXIV*, 1219; cf. Nolland, *Luke 18:35—24:43*, 904.

Robert F. O'Toole, classifies it as a quest story, whose main character, Zacchaeus, is portrayed as being on a quest to see Jesus and, thus, goes to great lengths to overcome obstacles that stand between him and Jesus.[16] Charles H. Talbert considers it as a conflict story similar to the pericope of Levi (Luke 5:27–32), where both pericopae have critics' grumbling at Jesus' association with sinners (Luke 5:30; 19:7).[17] Dennis Hamm describes it as a conversion story, parallel to the pericope of Levi and similar to the setting of the trilogy of the "lost" parables in Luke 15:1–32.[18] Richard C. White labels it as a vindication story because it lacks necessary characteristics of a salvation story, such as faith, sin, forgiveness, and repentance.[19] Last, but not least, Eugene LaVerdiere designates it as a hospitality story where the host, Zacchaeus, offers appropriate hospitality to Jesus, which may have included a meal and a nightly lodging at his house.[20] This survey should make it evident that the pericope of Zacchaeus, in its present Lukan form, lacks a pure definitive genre. François Bovon is correct in observing that this pericope appears to be an amalgamation, displaying "the characteristics of various literary genres; it can be viewed as a conversion, pardon, salvation, or controversy story."[21]

There is also no consensus among scholars with regard to the literary structure of the pericope of Zacchaeus. Some scholars, such as E. Earle Ellis, Darrell L. Bock, Eugene LaVerdiere, and James R. Edwards,[22] have diligently proposed conventional structural outlines for Luke 19:1–10, while others, such as Robert F. O'Toole and François Bovon, have suggested a diptych structure, divided into two complementary scenes hinged together by hook-words: the former's diptych outline is held together by Jesus' command to Zacchaeus and Zacchaeus's obedience to Jesus' command (Luke 19:5–6), while the latter's diptych diagram seems to be joined together by the presence and grumble of the crowd (Luke 19:3, 7).[23]

16. See Tannehill, *Luke*, 276; Tannehill, *Shape of Luke's Story*, 78; O'Toole, "Literary Form of Luke 19:1–10," 114, 116.

17. See Talbert, *Reading Luke*, 176–77.

18. See Hamm, "Luke 19:8," 436–37.

19. See White, "Vindication for Zacchaeus?," 21.

20. See LaVerdiere, *Dining in the Kingdom of God*, 107.

21. Bovon, *Luke 2*, 594; see also Bruehler, *Public and Political Christ*, 199.

22. See Ellis, *Gospel of Luke*, 221; Bock, *Luke 9:51—24:53*, 1515; LaVerdiere, *Dining in the Kingdom of God*, 107; Edwards, *Gospel According to Luke*, 529.

23. See O'Toole, "Literary Form of Luke 19:1–10," 112–16; Bovon, *Luke 2*, 593.

Although the pericope resists a neat and clear-cut outline, the following simplified proposed structure takes into consideration the two *mise en scènes* in the pericope. The exterior scene takes place in a public space in the town of Jericho; it consists of the first seven verses (Luke 19:1–7). The interior scene apparently happens in a private place inside the house of Zacchaeus; it includes the last three verses (Luke 19:8–10). Within this clear demarcation, the pericope can be additionally subdivided into sections, unfolding in the following fashion: (1) the setting (Luke 19:1), (2) Zacchaeus's appearance and actions (Luke 19:2–4), (3) Jesus' encounter with Zacchaeus and critics' grumbling (Luke 19:5–7), and (4) Zacchaeus's promissory declaration and Jesus' affirmation (Luke 19:8–10).

## Narrative Analysis

### The Setting (Luke 19:1)

The laconic introductory verse, Καὶ εἰσελθὼν διήρχετο τὴν Ἰεριχώ (*Kai eiselthōn diērcheto tēn Ierichō*, "And having entered, he was passing through Jericho," Luke 19:1), serves a double function. First, it explicitly provides a concrete and specific local setting for the pericope of Zacchaeus. In fact, the geographical reference to Jericho, as preserved in Luke 19:1, is rightly regarded by many scholars as pre-Lukan, meaning that the pericope of Zacchaeus was already set and located geographically in Jericho in Luke's "L" source.[24] While the subject of the aorist participle εἰσελθὼν (*eiselthōn*, "having entered") and the imperfect verb διήρχετο (*diērcheto*, "he was passing through") is unspecified, the flow of the narrative demands that it is Jesus. The evangelist is fond of the verb διέρχεσθαι (*dierchesthai*, "to go through," "to travel through"[25]) and uses it some thirty-one times in his two-volume work of Luke-Acts (e.g., Luke 2:15; 4:30; 8:22; 19:4; Acts 8:40; 9:32; 17:23; 18:23; 19:1). Second, it also narratively links this pericope closely with the preceding story of Jesus' healing of a blind beggar (Luke 18:35–43) by the repeated geographical reference to Jericho; in Luke 18:35, Jesus approaches Jericho, while in Luke 19:1, Jesus is in Jericho and is transiting through it. Thus, the entry into the new Hasmonean/Herodian city of

---

24. See Knox, *Sources of the Synoptic Gospels*, 2:111; Nolland, *Luke 18:35—24:43*, 904; Schweizer, *Good News According to Luke*, 290; Marshall, *Gospel of Luke*, 695–96; Fitzmyer, *Gospel According to Luke X–XXIV*, 1212; Bovon, *Luke 2*, 595–96.

25. See *BDAG*, 244.

Jericho brings Jesus' lengthy journey to Jerusalem, which has already begun in Luke 9:51, closer to its final destination. Unlike the evangelists Matthew and Mark, who, respectively, refer to Jericho once (Matt 20:29) and twice (Mark 10:46), Luke mentions it thrice (Luke 10:30; 18:35; 19:1), undoubtedly indicating his peculiar interest in the city.

### Zacchaeus's Appearance and Actions (Luke 19:2–4)

The evangelist employs the characteristic formula καὶ ἰδού (*kai idou*, "and behold," "and look," Luke 19:2) to focus attention on the entry of a new minor character, thus triggering a shift in the spotlight from Jesus to Zacchaeus, who is introduced with a significant amount of information.[26] In fact, Zacchaeus wears many different hats. His name is preceded by an unusual pleonastic locution of ἀνὴρ ὀνόματι καλούμενος (*anēr onomati kaloumenos*, "a man by name called [by name]," Luke 19:2), instead of simply ὀνόματι (*onomati*, "by name"[27]), as, for example, in Luke 1:5 and 23:50, or καλούμενος (*kaloumenos*, "called [by name]"[28]), as, for instance, in Acts 13:1 and 27:14. This redundant grammatical construction probably attempts to draw attention to the meaning of the name itself.[29] Etymologically, the name Ζακχαῖος (*Zakchaios*, "Zacchaeus"), with its different spelling variations (Ζακχος, *Zakchos* [LXX books of Ezra 2:9 and Neh 7:14]; Σακχαῖος, *Sakchaios* [*Life* 46 §239]), is the Graecized form of the Hebrew name זַכַּי (*Zakkay*), meaning "pure" "innocent," and "righteous."[30] Zacchaeus's name, which is itself a likely indication that he was a Jewish man (Luke 19:9), does not have any symbolic value or function in the pericope. However, the inclusion of his personal name may strongly indicate that he would have been known in the early Christian community in Jerusalem where the pericope in which he is named was first told from the perspective of Zacchaeus himself.[31]

26. See Yamasaki, "Point of View," 98–99.

27. See *BDAG*, 711–14.

28. See *BDAG*, 502–4.

29. See Nolland, *Luke 18:35—24:43*, 904; Bovon, *Luke 2*, 596; Metzger, *Consumption and Wealth*, 171.

30. See *BDB*, 269.

31. See Bauckham, *Jesus and the Eyewitnesses*, 46, 55. According to the *Pseudo-Clementine Literature*, dated to the fourth century, Zacchaeus welcomes and hosts Simon Peter upon his arrival in the coastal city of Caesarea (*Ps.-Clem. Rec.* 1:73) and is later ordained by

Zacchaeus's occupation as ἀρχιτελώνης (*architelōnēs*, "chief toll collector," Luke 19:2[32]), a *hapax legomenon*, points to his ability to climb to the top of the socioeconomic ladder of success. From a career point of view, he would have been a well-established entrepreneur and contractor, who succeeded in leasing from Rome, or its political representatives, the right of collecting indirect taxes, such as tolls, customs, and tariffs. He would have then subcontracted it to other local Jewish toll collectors, who, in turn, sat at toll booths near city gates (cf. Luke 5:27), collecting taxes and dues on all trade imported and exported from Galilee and Perea to Judea, and vice versa. Such a career, however, came with a heavy price tag since toll collectors and their chiefs were looked upon by the majority of the first-century Jewish population as quislings of the Roman occupation, oppression, subordination, and domination. They were suspected of dishonesty, rapacity, and cruelty in extracting extra money from their fellow citizens to enrich themselves (cf. Luke 3:12–13). It is no accident that Zacchaeus is described as πλούσιος (*plousios*, "wealthy," "rich," Luke 19:2[33]). His affluence must have been generated from his entrepreneurship of collecting indirect taxes in excess for personal gain.[34] The occupation of collecting indirect taxes was also considered degrading and repugnant (*b. Sanh.* 25b) and those who practiced it experienced ignominy and ostracism. They were viewed as sinners and ritually unclean (Luke 19:7).[35] It seems that first-century Jewish courts did not admit toll collectors as witnesses in any lawsuit or case. One of Jesus' closest disciples, Levi, who is also identified as Matthew (Luke 5:27; Mark 2:14; Matt 9:9; 10:3), had previously worked as a toll collector at the toll booth in Capernaum for the regime of Herod Antipas, who ruled Galilee and Perea between 4 BCE–39 CE (*Ant.* 17.11.4 §§317–18). It should be clear by now that there is a hint of irony or satire between the meaning of Zacchaeus's name and his occupation.

That Zacchaeus is described as wealthy likely draws an unfavorable critical reaction from Luke's audience. Up to this moment in the Gospel

---

him, though against his will, as bishop of that city (*Ps.-Clem. Hom.* 3:63, 3:66).

32. See *BDAG*, 139.

33. See *BDAG*, 831.

34. See Fitzmyer, *Gospel According to Luke X–XXIV*, 1213; Bock, *Luke 9:51—24:53*, 1516; Green, *Gospel of Luke*, 668.

35. See Schürer, *History of the Jewish People*, 1:372–76; Jeremias, *Jerusalem in the Time of Jesus*, 32, 310–12; Donahue, "Tax Collectors and Sinners," 39–61; Sanders, *Jesus and Judaism*, 178; Perkins, "Taxes in the New Testament," 182–200; Derrett, *Law in the New Testament*, 281.

narrative, Luke has clearly portrayed the wealthy in a negative light because their money-centric attitude, viz., acquisition of and attachment to wealth, becomes an obstacle hindering them from entering the kingdom of God, as well as responding to the call of discipleship. In fact, at the very outset, Mary discloses in the Magnificat that the wealthy are sent away empty (Luke 1:53). As far back as the Beatitudes, Jesus utters a woe upon the wealthy (Luke 6:24). This antithesis is particularly conspicuous in Jesus' parables of the wealthy fool (Luke 12:13–21) and the wealthy man and Lazarus (Luke 16:19–31). Furthermore, Jesus' encounter with the wealthy ruler shows how the latter is incapable of responding to Jesus' invitation to discipleship because of his ineptitude to divest himself of his material wealth in order to assist the poor (Luke 18:18–30). Will Zacchaeus change his allegiance from trusting material wealth to trusting God? There is a flickering glimpse of hope (Luke 18:27).

Jesus' passing through the city of Jericho, with the crowd accompanying him (Luke 18:39), gets the attention of Zacchaeus, who is now depicted as ἐζήτει ἰδεῖν τὸν Ἰησοῦν τίς ἐστιν (ezētei idein ton Iēsoun tes estin, "he was seeking to see who Jesus is," Luke 19:3). It is unclear as to what motivates him to do so. Curiosity? In all probability, it would seem that some encouraging and remarkable reports of Levi's conversion and response to Jesus' invitation to discipleship (Luke 5:27), Jesus' association with toll collectors and sinners (Luke 5:30; 7:34; 15:1), and Jesus' healing of the blind beggar (Luke 18:35–43) may have reached Zacchaeus's ears. However, he is unable to reach Jesus and catch a glimpse of him because two major obstacles lie directly in the way. First, ἀπὸ τοῦ ὄχλου (apo tou ochlou, "because of the crowd," Luke 19:3) indicates that the density of the crowd surrounding Jesus is high (cf. Luke 8:19), creating a sort of human barrier completely obstructing Zacchaeus's sight. The obstruction of the large crowd, which Zacchaeus, a man of substance and prominence, is incapable of penetrating, is not merely physical, but also social: the crowd determines, on moral grounds (Luke 19:7), to deny him the privilege of seeing Jesus,[36] just as the crowd has attempted, in the context immediately preceding the pericope of Zacchaeus, to block the access of a blind beggar to Jesus (Luke 18:39). Second, ἡλικίᾳ μικρὸς ἦν (hēlikia mikros ēn, "he [Zacchaeus] was short in stature," Luke 19:3) makes it difficult for Zacchaeus to look over the crowd. This reference to Zacchaeus's diminutive size would have incited ridicule

---

36. See Nolland, *Luke 18:35—24:43*, 905, 908; Green, *Gospel of Luke*, 670; Carroll, *Luke*, 372.

from ancient audiences because it was associated with small-mindedness and greediness.[37] The contrast between the large size of the crowd and the physical description of Zacchaeus is certainly ironic.

Undeterred, Zacchaeus goes to great lengths just to get a glimpse of Jesus. He runs forward to the front of the crowd's procession, climbs into a sycamore tree, and perches himself on its branches, thus placing himself in a spot where he may get the chance to see Jesus as he is about to pass through that way. The expression, προδραμὼν εἰς τὸ ἔμπροσθεν (prodramōn eis to emprosthen, "having run on ahead into the front," Luke 19:4), is another pleonastic construction. However, no matter how ridiculous, undignified, and shameful his actions would have been viewed in first-century Palestine, Zacchaeus is on a quest to see Jesus. The seriousness of his curiosity "conceals an unconscious yearning to see God."[38] Beyond Luke 19:4, the compound verb προτρέχειν (protrechein, "to run on ahead"[39]) also appears in John 20:4 with reference to the other disciple outrunning Peter to the site of Jesus' empty tomb. This kind of sycamore tree (1 Kgs 10:27; Amos 7:14; Ps 78:47), which grew up in Palestine during Jesus' time, was like an oak tree (Luke 17:6), easy to climb because of its short trunk and wide branches.

## Jesus' Encounter with Zacchaeus and Critics' Grumbling (Luke 19:5–7)

The turning point of the narrative, as well as the turning point in Zacchaeus's life, happens when Jesus comes to the place beneath the sycamore tree in which Zacchaeus is perched. The entire procession is now brought to a sudden halt. Looking upward (ἀναβλέψας, anablepsas, "having looked up," Luke 19:5), Jesus spots the wealthy chief toll collector in the sycamore tree. Zacchaeus, who has hoped to catch sight of Jesus, is seen first by him. So powerful is this vertical moment in time: Jesus looks up while Zacchaeus looks down. They exchange glances and, probably, smile. Moreover, they exchange roles: the seeker—Zacchaeus—immediately becomes the sought, and the one who is sought—Jesus—becomes the seeker. Jesus then takes the initiative to reach out to Zacchaeus. He addresses him by his personal name and summons him to hurry and come down from the sycamore tree, thus bringing him from the circumference to the center. Jesus' knowledge of Zacchaeus's name recalls his supernatural knowledge of Nathanael's name

37. See further Parsons, "'Short in Stature,'" 50–57.

38. Schweizer, Good News According to Luke, 291.

39. See BDAG, 889.

in John 1:47–48.[40] In an unprecedented way, Jesus invites himself into Zacchaeus's house to be his guest for some length of time: σήμερον γὰρ ἐν τῷ οἴκῳ σου δεῖ με μεῖναι (*sēmeron gar en tō oikō sou dei me meinai*, "for today it is necessary for me to stay at your house," Luke 19:5). This verse is packed with two important Lukan terms. The adverb σήμερον (*sēmeron*, "today," "this very day"[41]), which also appears in Luke 19:9, is employed to heighten the immediacy and imminence of divine activity whose objective is salvific (Luke 2:11; 4:21; 5:25; 13:32; 23:43).[42] The impersonal verb δεῖ (*dei*, "it is necessary," "one must"[43]), which carries a wide range of meaning (Luke 2:49; 4:43; 9:22; 22:37; 24:26), is used here to convey Jesus' fulfillment and accomplishment of divine commission and mission.[44]

Καὶ σπεύσας κατέβη καὶ ὑπεδέξατο αὐτὸν χαίρων (*Kai speusas katebē kai hypedexato auton chairōn*, "And, having hurried, he came down and received him rejoicing," Luke 19:6) shows how Zacchaeus responds with conformity and alacrity to Jesus' command. Luke's use of the verb σπεύδειν (*speudein*, "to hurry," "to hasten," Luke 19:6[45]) to describe Zacchaeus's celerity echoes the hurried movement of the shepherds to find baby Jesus (Luke 2:16). In both cases, there is a sense of urgency (cf. Luke 1:39). The verb ὑποδέχεσθαι (*hypodechesthai*, "to welcome," "to entertain as a guest," Luke 19:6[46]) is used to report Zacchaeus's hospitable reception of Jesus (cf. Luke 10:38; Acts 17:7; Jas 2:25), which would have included a meal and a nightly lodging at his house. Zacchaeus is getting more than he expected and anticipated. Jesus' self-invitation into Zacchaeus's house undoubtedly has an enormous psychological impact on Zacchaeus, whose internal disposition is outwardly expressed with a sense of joyful exaltation. The verb χαίρειν (*chairein*, "to rejoice," "to be glad," Luke 19:6[47]) is etymologically related to the noun χάρις (*charis*, "grace," "graciousness," "gratitude"[48]). Zacchaeus's delighted response to Jesus' self-invitation is, therefore, an act

40. See Fitzmyer, *Gospel According to Luke X–XXIV*, 1214; Bovon, *Luke 2*, 598; Nolland, *Luke 18:35—24:43*, 905.

41. See *BDAG*, 921.

42. See Loewe "Towards an Interpretation," 325.

43. See *BDAG*, 213–14.

44. See Cosgrove, "Divine Δεῖ," 175; Tannehill, *Shape of Luke's Story*, 77.

45. See *BDAG*, 937–38.

46. See *BDAG*, 1037.

47. See *BDAG*, 1074–75.

48. See *BDAG*, 1079–81.

of grace. As François Bovon elegantly points out, "The fact that Zacchaeus opened the door to his house with joy reflects a conviction on the part of the Gospel writer that God's presence inevitably gladdens the human heart."[49] The motif of joy permeates the Gospel (e.g., Luke 1:14; 2:10; 6:23; 8:13; 10:20; 13:17; 15:7, 10, 32). The joyful response of Zacchaeus to Jesus is a striking contrast to the sorrowful response (περίλυπος, *perilypos*, "deeply grieved") of the anonymous rich ruler (Luke 18:23).

Zacchaeus's sense of rejoicing is, however, overshadowed by the negative reaction of the collective conscience of πάντες (*pantes*, "everyone," "all," Luke 19:7[50]). The same crowd that has earlier obstructed Zacchaeus from catching a glimpse of Jesus is now pejoratively grumbling at the sight of Jesus going to lodge with Zacchaeus, who is described by them as a ἁμαρτωλῷ ἀνδρὶ (*hamartōlō andri*, "a sinful man," Luke 19:7). As a chief toll collector, Zacchaeus's sinfulness naturally derives from his political loyalty to Rome.[51] Everyone in the crowd, including disciples and opponents,[52] disapproves of Jesus' entry into Zacchaeus's house, thus displaying imperceptiveness about Jesus' mission as expressed in the Nazareth manifesto (cf. Luke 4:16–21). The grumbling of the crowd unmistakably recalls the grumbling of the Pharisees and the scribes about Jesus' association with toll collectors and sinners (Luke 5:30; 15:2). The juxtaposition between Zacchaeus's rejoicing and the crowd's grumbling is another apparent irony.

*Zacchaeus's Promissory Declaration and*
*Jesus' Affirmation (Luke 19:8–10)*

Although no meal is explicitly mentioned in the pericope of Zacchaeus (cf. Luke 10:38–42), Luke's earlier use of μένειν (*menein*, "to stay," Luke 19:5[53]), ὑποδέχεσθαι (*hypodechesthai*, "to welcome," "to entertain as a guest," Luke 19:6), and καταλύειν (*katalyein*, "to lodge," Luke 19:7[54]) strongly imply a meal would be shared.[55] What follows is, therefore, read within the context of sharing a table-fellowship and hospitality.

49. Bovon, *Luke 2*, 598.

50. See *BDAG*, 782–84.

51. See Levine and Witherington, *Gospel of Luke*, 511.

52. See Johnson, *Gospel of Luke*, 285.

53. See *BDAG*, 630–31.

54. See *BDAG*, 521–22.

55. See Hamm, "Luke 19:8," 435; Hamm, "Zacchaeus Revisited," 250; LaVerdiere,

At some point during the meal, Zacchaeus stands up from reclining at the table (σταθεὶς, *statheis*, "having stood up," Luke 19:8) to deliver a promissory declaration. He speaks directly to Jesus and addresses him as κύριε (*kyrie*, "Lord," "sir," "master"), thus displaying faith in him, like Peter (Luke 5:8), the leper (Luke 5:12), the centurion (Luke 7:6), the seventy disciples (Luke 10:17), Martha (Luke 10:40), and the blind man (Luke 18:41). Everyone in the banquet room turns and looks at their host standing at the head of the table. Having attracted the attention of all diners, Zacchaeus exclaims: Ἰδοὺ τὰ ἡμίσιά μου τῶν ὑπαρχόντων, κύριε, τοῖς πτωχοῖς δίδωμι, καὶ εἴ τινός τι ἐσυκοφάντησα ἀποδίδωμι τετραπλοῦν (*Idou ta hēmisia mou tōn hyparchontōn, kyrie, tois ptōchois didōmi, kai ei tinos ti esykophantēsa apodidōmi tetraploun*, "Behold, half of my possessions, Lord, I am giving to the poor, and if I have extorted anything of anyone, I am giving back fourfold," Luke 19:8).

What motivates Zacchaeus to make such a voluntarily spontaneous and remarkable announcement? It is not far-fetched to suggest that the answer lies with Jesus' welcoming presence and acceptance of Zacchaeus. The two present indicative active verbs in Zacchaeus's speech (διδόναι, *didonai*, "to give," and ἀποδιδόναι, *apodidonai*, "to give back," Luke 19:8) are translated here into the futuristic present to reflect Zacchaeus's radical *metanoia* as a result of encountering Jesus. If these verbs were rendered into the iterative or customary present to express Zacchaeus's regular acts of charity and compensation, it would then be difficult to envision why the crowd would hold him in contempt by labeling him as a sinner (Luke 19:7). Zacchaeus's ethical transformation, nonetheless, has two components. First, in contrast to the rich male characters in Luke's Gospel (Luke 12:13–21; 16:19–31; 18:18–25), Zacchaeus resolves to divest himself of half of his wealth and philanthropically give it to the poor to probably alleviate poverty. Second, with the other half of his wealth, he legally pledges to make fourfold restitution to whomsoever he has wrongfully and unlawfully exacted money (cf. Exod 21:37 [MT] = Exod 22:1 [LXX]; 2 Sam 12:5–6; *Ant.* 16.1.1 §3). The first-class conditional clause, ". . . and if I have extorted anything of anyone," makes it clear that Zacchaeus is culpable of extortion and malpractices.[56] Zacchaeus's promissory declaration implies

---

*Dining in the Kingdom of God,* 107; Just, *Ongoing Feast,* 188; Karris, *Eating Your Way through Luke's Gospel,* 36.

56. See Plummer, *Critical and Exegetical Commentary,* 435; Schweizer, *Good News According to Luke,* 292; Marshall, *Gospel of Luke,* 698; Ellis, *Gospel of Luke,* 221; Bock, *Luke 9:51—24:53,* 1521; Carroll, *Luke,* 371, 373.

the presence of faith which bears fruits worthy of repentance (Luke 3:8), thus exemplifying the message of John the Baptist (Luke 3:12–14). The decisive turning point of the pericope has been reached: Zacchaeus's change of heart and transformation of character. His radical repentance is a concrete sign that God's kingdom, as historically inaugurated by Jesus, has been actualized in world history (cf. Luke 12:32–34).

Jesus' asseveration of Zacchaeus's promissory declaration has a double function. First, Jesus directly speaks to Zacchaeus and proclaims to him that today σωτηρία τῷ οἴκῳ τούτῳ ἐγένετο (sōtēria tō oikō toutō egeneto, "salvation has come to this house," Luke 19:9). This salvation, rooted in a historical event, has social and spiritual nuances and consequences (Luke 1:69, 71, 77; 2:30–31). The evangelist is fond of narrating household conversions in his two-volume work of Luke-Acts: Zacchaeus the chief toll collector at Jericho (Luke 19:1–10), Cornelius the Roman centurion at Caesarea (Acts 10:1—11:18), Lydia of Thyatira at Philippi (Acts 16:13–15, 40), the anonymous Roman jailer at Philippi (Acts 16:16–34), and Crispus the synagogue leader at Corinth (Acts 18:7–8; 1 Cor 1:14). John's Gospel has one household conversion: the royal official at Capernaum (John 4:46–54). Second, Jesus speaks of Zacchaeus in the third person, addressing all the diners in the banquet room and reminding them that Zacchaeus is also a son of Abraham. This recalls Luke 13:10–17, where Jesus speaks of a crippled woman, whom he heals on the Sabbath, in the third person, telling the indignant synagogue leader and his followers that she is a daughter of Abraham. The patriarch Abraham, who probably lived during the early nineteenth/late eighteenth century BCE, and whose life is narrated in Genesis 11:26—25:11, is the recipient of God's covenant and promises. He is also the spiritual founder of Judaism. As a descendant of Abraham, Zacchaeus's ignominious occupation, which has previously marginalized him from the Jewish community in Jericho (Luke 19:3, 7), does not negate the promises God has made to Abraham and his descendants (Luke 1:54–55; 73–74). Jesus acknowledges the validity of Zacchaeus's promissory declaration as bearing fruits of repentance, thus rehabilitating him as a son of Abraham (Luke 3:7–9).[57] Zacchaeus's membership in God's kingdom has been restored. He is "a camel," so to speak, who has entered God's kingdom through "the eye of a needle" (Luke 18:24–25). Jesus' asseveration of

---

57. See Derrett, *Law in the New Testament*, 285; Karris, *Eating Your Way through Luke's Gospel*, 37.

salvation in Luke 19:9 is inextricably connected to Zacchaeus's promissory declaration in Luke 19:8.

The pericope comes to a close with a description of Jesus' salvific mission: ἦλθεν γὰρ ὁ υἱὸς τοῦ ἀνθρώπου ζητῆσαι καὶ σῶσαι τὸ ἀπολωλός (*elthen gar ho huios tou anthrōpou zētēsai kai sōsai to apolōlos*, "for the Son of Man came to seek out and to save the lost," Luke 19:10). Jesus' self-designation as ὁ υἱὸς τοῦ ἀνθρώπου (*ho huios tou anthrōpou*, "the son of the man," Luke 19:10) can only be understood as a translation of the Aramaic בַּר (אֱ)נָשָׁא (*bar [ʾĕ]nāšāʾ*, "the son of man"). The origin of this designation surfaces for the first time in the Aramaic section of the book of Daniel (Dan 2:4—7:28), where the seer sees כְּבַר אֱנָשׁ (*kĕbar ʾĕnāš*, "one like a son of man," Dan 7:13), coming on the clouds of heaven, led into God's presence, and granted eternal dominion, glory, and kingship (cf. 2 Esd 13:3, 25–26, 32, 37–39; 1 En. 46:1–4; 48:2; 61:10–13). In the New Testament, Jesus is implicitly and explicitly identified and referred to as the Danielic human-like figure (Mark 13:26; 14:62; John 5:26–27; 9:35–38; Rev 1:7, 12–16).[58] Statistically speaking, Luke uses the Son of Man designation twenty-six times in his two-volume work of Luke-Acts: twenty-four instances come from the lips of Jesus (Luke 5:24; 6:5, 22; 7:34; 9:22, 26, 44, 58; 11:30; 12:8, 10, 40; 17:22, 24, 26, 30; 18:8, 31; 19:10; 21:27, 36; 22:22, 48, 69), and two more come from the mouths of the two angelic beings and Stephen, respectively (Luke 24:7; Acts 7:56). The Son of Man designation cannot only be understood as a circumlocutional reference to the speaker.[59] In the context of Luke's Gospel, it functions as a christological title with distinct nuances and connotations.[60] Following Rudolf Bultmann,[61] Luke's Son of Man sayings can be divided into three categories, dealing with (1) Jesus' earthly ministry (e.g., Luke 5:24; 7:34; 9:58; 12:10; 19:10), (2) Jesus' passion-death-resurrection (e.g., Luke 9:22, 44; 18:31; 24:7), and (3) Jesus' exaltation (e.g., Luke 9:26; 12:8; 17:24; 21:27; 22:69).

In Luke 19:10, the evangelist fittingly summarizes the mission of Jesus in terms of coming to seek and save the lost. There is a strong verbal

---

58. See further Moule, *Origin of Christology*, 11–22; Marshall, "Synoptic 'Son of Man,'" 132–50.

59. For further discussion, see Vermes, *Jesus the Jew*, 160–91; Fitzmyer, *Wandering Aramean*, 143–60; Donahue, "Recent Studies," 484–98; Collins, "Origin of the Designation of Jesus," 391–407.

60. See further Cullmann, *Christology of the New Testament*, 137–92; O'Toole, *Luke's Presentation of Jesus*, 141–54.

61. See Bultmann, *Theology of the New Testament*, 30.

connection between the two pericopae of Levi (Luke 5:27–32) and Zacchaeus (Luke 19:1–10); in the former, Jesus declares that ἐλήλυθα (*elēlytha*, "I have come," Luke 5:32) to call sinners to repentance, while in the latter, he states that he ἦλθεν (*ēlthen*, "came," Luke 19:10) to seek and save the lost. Both verses certainly underscore Jesus' gracious attitude toward the social and religious outcasts of his day. In a wonderful twist of irony, Zacchaeus, who "was seeking to see who Jesus is" (Luke 19:3), ends up now hearing from Jesus himself that the whole purpose of the Son of Man's salvific mission is "to seek and save the lost" (Luke 19:10).[62] That Zacchaeus is described as ἀπολωλός (*apolōlos*, "lost," Luke 19:10[63]) recalls Jesus' three parables of the "lost" coin, sheep, and son in Luke 15:3–32. There is joy in finding the lost. Furthermore, Ezekiel employs the shepherd metaphor to portray Yahweh, the God of Israel, as faithfully seeking the lost sheep of Israel. Thus, Yahweh, after criticizing Israel's shepherds for neglecting the flock entrusted to them and not seeking the sheep that have gone astray and were lost, personally promises to intervene and seek the lost and bring back the strayed sheep (Ezek 34:16). There is a continuation between Yahweh's mission and Jesus' mission (cf. Luke 15:3–7).

62. See Tannehill, *Luke*, 278; Tannehill, *Shape of Luke's Story*, 77.
63. See *BDAG*, 115–16.

# 6

# "Do You Desire To Become Healthy?"

## Text

1 After this there was a festival of the Jews, and Jesus went up to Jerusalem. 2 Now in Jerusalem by the Sheep Gate there is a pool, called in Hebrew Beth-zatha, which has five porticoes. 3 In these lay many invalids - blind, lame, and paralyzed. 5 One man was there who had been ill for thirty-eight years. 6 When Jesus saw him lying there and knew that he had been there a long time, he said to him, "Do you want to be made well?" 7 The sick man answered him, "Sir, I have no one to put me into the pool when the water is stirred up; and while I am making my way, someone else steps down ahead of me." 8 Jesus said to him, "Stand up, take your mat and walk." 9 At once the man was made well, and he took up his mat and began to walk. Now that day was a sabbath. 10 So the Jews said to the man who had been cured, "It is the sabbath; it is not lawful for you to carry your mat." 11 But he answered them, "The man who made me well said to me, 'Take up your mat and walk.'" 12 They asked him, "Who is the man who said to you, 'Take it up and walk?'" 13 Now the man who had been healed did not know who it was, for Jesus had disappeared in the crowd that was there. 14 Later Jesus found him in the temple and said to him, "See, you have been made well! Do not sin any more, so that nothing worse happens to you." 15 The man went away and told the Jews that it was Jesus who had made him well. 16 Therefore the Jews started persecuting Jesus, because he was doing such things on the sabbath. 17 But Jesus answered them, "My Father is still working, and I also am working." 18 For this reason the Jews were seeking all the more to kill him, because he was not only breaking the sabbath, but was also calling God his own Father, thereby making himself equal to God.

John 5:1–18 (NRSV)[1]

1. The pericope of John 5:1–18, or John 5:1–3a, 5–16, is liturgically read on the fourth

## Scholarly Context

IT HAS BEEN LONG recognized that John's Gospel stands thematically quite apart from the Synoptic Gospels in many ways. Although the evangelist had access to sources associated with the Synoptic traditions,[2] as evidenced, for example, by the inclusion of certain amount of materials into the Gospel, such as the feeding of the five thousand (John 6:1–13 ‖ Mark 6:30–44 ‖ Matt 14:13–21 ‖ Luke 9:10–17), the walking on water (John 6:16–21 ‖ Mark 6:45–52 ‖ Matt 14:22–33), the anointing at Bethany (John 12:1–8 ‖ Mark 14:3–9 ‖ Matt 26:6–13), and the passion and death (John 18–19 ‖ Mark 14–15 ‖ Matt 26–27 ‖ Luke 22–23), there remains no consensus in Johannine scholarship regarding the precise identification of other distinct and unique sources of information, independent of the Synoptic Gospels, the evangelist used and edited to fit his own historical, theological, and christological narrative about Jesus' life. It seems reasonable to date the final edition of John's Gospel between 90–100 CE.[3]

In his 1941 German commentary on John's Gospel, Rudolf Bultmann postulated that one of the literary purported sources at the disposal of the evangelist was a σημεῖα (sēmeia, "signs") source, an early independent collection of miracles, supposedly written in Semitizing/Aramaizing Greek style of composition.[4] This hypothetical source, no longer extant, probably included all the seven miraculous works of Jesus (John 2:1–12; 4:43–54; 5:1–16; 6:1–14, 16–21; 9:1–39; 11:1–44), dispersed throughout the first half of the Gospel (John 1:19—12:50), which is often referred to by scholars as the book of Signs.[5] Strikingly, only the first two signs of Jesus' miraculous deeds, viz., the pericope of changing water into wine (John 2:1–12) and the pericope of the healing of the royal official's son (John 4:46–54), which both take place in Cana of Galilee (John 2:1; 4:46), are enumerated (John 2:11; 4:54). It is obvious that the purpose of the σημεῖα (sēmeia) source "was to demonstrate that Jesus," writes Dwight Moody Smith, "was the expected

---

week Tuesday Mass of Lent.

2. See further Barrett, *Gospel According to St. John*, 42–54; Kysar, *John*, 9–13.

3. See, for example, Brown, *Gospel According to John (I–XII)*, lxxxiv.

4. See Bultmann, *Gospel of John*, 6–7, 238.

5. For other materials assigned by Rudolf Bultmann to the σημεῖα-source, such as John 1:35–51; 4:1–42; 7:1–13; 10:40–42; 12:37–38; 20:30–31, see further Smith, *Composition and Order*, 34–43; Kysar, *Voyages with John*, 62.

Messiah by displaying his miraculous power"[6] in order to evoke faith (cf. John 2:23; 12:37–38; 20:30–31).

Unlike the first two signs of Jesus' miraculous works in Cana of Galilee, which are visibly brief and self-contained, the pericope of the healing of the lame man at the pool of Bethesda in Jerusalem (John 5:1–18), in its present state, forms part of the larger literary context of John 5 and 7. It contains pre-Johannine elements probably derived from the σημεῖα (sēmeia) source (e.g., John 5:2–3, 5–9, 14). It has no precise parallel in the Synoptic Gospels. Nevertheless, it raises several intriguing problems. In its present canonical order in John 5, it can be sequentially enumerated as Jesus' third miraculous sign. However, if one tentatively accepts Rudolf Bultmann's transposition and rearrangement hypothesis of John 5, 6, and 7,[7] two conclusions, then, become inevitable: (1) the pericope of the healing of the lame man at the pool of Bethesda would have been Jesus' fifth miraculous sign, probably connected to the healing of the blind man in John 9, which both take place in Jerusalem; and (2) John 5 would immediately have been followed by John 7:15–24, which clearly has elements referring directly back to the controversy surrounding the healing-on-the-Sabbath pericope in John 5:1–18.[8] Briefly stated, the main argument for the transposition of John 5 and 6 seems to improve John's geographical itinerary of Jesus. Consider these two examples. First, John 6:1 mentions that Jesus is near the Sea of Galilee. This geographical reference links up seamlessly with the ending of John 4:54, where Jesus is still in Cana of Galilee. Second, John 7:1 says that οἱ Ἰουδαῖοι (hoi Ioudaioi, "the Judeans," "the Jews") are looking for an opportunity to kill Jesus. This would only make sense after John 5:17–18. However, one valid objection to this transposition and rearrangement hypothesis is the lack of manuscript evidence.

The spelling of the name of the pool is beset with difficulty. It appears in various renderings in the manuscripts. First, Βηθσαϊδά (Bēthsaida, "Bethsaida," meaning "house/place of fishing/hunting") has the strongest attestation (P66 [ca. 200 CE], P75 [ca. 175–225 CE], B [ca. 350 CE], and Jerome's Latin Vulgate [ca. 384 CE]).[9] Most scholars, however, exclude it as merely a scribal assimilation to the town of Bethsaida on the Sea of

---

6. Smith, *Johannine Christianity*, 86.

7. See Bultmann, *Gospel of John*, 10, 209–10, 237–39.

8. See also Barrett, *Gospel According to St. John*, 23; Nicol, *Sēmeia in the Fourth Gospel*, 6; Schnackenburg, *Gospel According to St. John*, 2:90–91.

9. The reading of Bethsaida is accepted by Michaels, *Gospel of John*, 289.

Galilee (cf. John 1:44; 12:21). Second, Βηθζαθά (*Bēthzatha,* "Bethzatha," meaning "house/place of olive orchard") is the least unsatisfactory reading (ℵ [ca. 375 CE] and D [ca. 450 CE]).[10] It most likely refers to the region just north of the Jerusalem Temple, which is called either Bethzaith (1 Macc 7:19), or Bezetha/Bethzetho (*J.W.* 5.5.8 § 246; *Ant.* 12.10.2 §397).[11] Third, Βηθεσδά (*Bēthesda,* "Bethesda," meaning "house/place of mercy") has the weakest attestation (A [ca. 450 CE] and C [ca. 450 CE]). It is the most likely reading preferred by many scholars today,[12] especially in view of the discovery of the Copper Scroll at Qumran, which reads in Hebrew "Bet-Eshdatain" (3Q15 11:11–12).[13] The ending of the Hebrew name is dual, indicating the probable existence of twin pools. It seems to be derived from the Aramaic singular noun Bet-Eshda ("house of the flowing," "place of poured-out [water]").[14]

The pericope of the healing of the lame man at the pool of Bethesda in Jerusalem has another particular textual problem. A cursory reading shows that there is a gap between John 5:3 and John 5:5. A variety of less important manuscripts have either a short addition, "... waiting for the stirring of the water" (John 5:3b NRSV) or a longer addition, "... for an angel of the Lord went down at certain seasons into the pool, and stirred up the water; whoever stepped in first after the stirring of the water was made well from whatever disease that person had" (John 5:4 NRSV). Notice that while the NRSV and NIV have the missing verses of John 5:3b–4 in the footnote, KJV and NASB have them in the text itself. Most Johannine scholars regard John 5:3b–4 to be interpolated glosses, added later by scribes to provide an explanation for John 5:7.[15] The textual excision of John 5:3b–4 seems justified due to its absence from the earliest and most reliable extant Greek papyri and uncial codices (e.g., P66, P75, ℵ, B, and

---

10. This reading is favored by Bultmann, *Gospel of John,* 240; *GNT,* 329; NRSV; RSV.

11. See Charlesworth, *Jesus as Mirrored in John,* 188–89.

12. See Barrett, *Gospel According to St. John,* 252–53; Schnackenburg, *Gospel According to St. John,* 2:94; Moloney, *Gospel of John,* 172; Keener, *Gospel of John,* 1:636; Wahlde, "Archaeology and John's Gospel," 560–61; Perkins, "Gospel According to John," 959.

13. See Vermes, *Complete Dead Sea Scrolls in English,* 588.

14. See Brown, *Gospel According to John (I–XII),* 207; Metzger, *Textual Commentary,* 208.

15. See Bultmann, *Gospel of John,* 241; Dodd, *Historical Tradition,* 179; Barrett, *Gospel According to St. John,* 253; Brown, *Gospel According to John (I–XII),* 207; Schnackenburg, *Gospel According to St. John,* 2:95; Moloney, *Gospel of John,* 171; Michaels, *Gospel of John,* 290; Haenchen, *John 1,* 46.

C), as well as the presence of a number of *hapax legomena*, such as κίνησιν (*kinēsin*, "moving," "stirring," John 5:3b) and νοσήματι (*nosēmati*, "disease," John 5:4).[16] At any rate, one thing seems to be certain: the scribes who inserted John 5:3b–4 into the pericope of the healing of the lame man at the pool of Bethesda in Jerusalem to explain John 5:7 might have intended to attribute the therapeutic properties and qualities of its waters to a divine intervention, viz., "an angel of the Lord" (John 5:4).

## Literary Genre and Structure

The unit of the healing-on-the-Sabbath controversy pericope (John 5:1–18) is unmistakably a mixture of two literary genres: a healing-miracle story itself (John 5:2–3, 5–9, 14) and a Sabbath controversy (John 5:10–13, 15–18). The healing itself, which becomes the occasion for the controversy with the Judeans over the Sabbath, follows the classic threefold pattern typical of all such miracles. First, the *description of disease* provides a succinct account of the patient's illness: the lame man has been ill for thirty-eight years (John 5:5). Second, the *healing of disease* shows that the patient's illness is uniquely restored and corrected by the miracle-worker: Jesus commands the lame man to stand up, carry his mat, and walk (John 5:8). Third, the *proof of healing* authenticates the success of the miracle itself: the lame man is healed, carries his mat, and begins to walk (John 5:9). The healing-miracle story, furthermore, contains a combination of at least thirteen literary motifs found in Jewish and pagan miracle stories of antiquity.[17] They are as follows:

1. The Coming of the Miracle-Worker (". . . and Jesus went up to Jerusalem," John 5:1).

2. The Appearance of the Crowd (". . . a crowd being in the place," John 5:13).

3. The Appearance of the Distressed Person (". . . a certain man," John 5:5).

4. The Appearance of the Opponents (". . . the Judeans," John 5:10, 15, 16).

---

16. See *GNT*, 330; Metzger, *Textual Commentary*, 208; Fee, "On the Inauthenticity of John 5:3b–4," 207–18.

17. See Theissen, *Miracle Stories*, 47–72.

5. Description of the Distress (". . . having been thirty-eight years in his infirmity," John 5:5).

6. Difficulties in the Approach ("Sir, I have no man . . ." John 5:7).

7. Misunderstanding ("Sir, I have no man that he might put me into the pool when the water has been stirred," John 5:7).

8. Criticism of the Opponents ("It is sabbath, and it is not permitted for you to take up your mat," John 5:10).

9. The Withdrawal of the Miracle-Worker (". . . for Jesus had quietly withdrawn," John 5:13).

10. Miracle-Working Word ("Arise, take up your mat and walk," John 5:8).

11. Recognition of the Miracle (". . . and immediately the man became healthy," John 5:9).

12. Demonstration (". . . and he took up his mat and was walking," John 5:9).

13. Rejection ("Who is the man having said to you, 'Take up and walk?'" John 5:12).

As a subcategory of Rudolf Bultmann's apophthegms, the Sabbath-controversy story has a basic literary form comprising a threefold pattern characteristic of rabbinic discussion.[18] First, the starting point lies in some action or attitude: Jesus heals the lame man on the Sabbath (John 5:5–9). Second, the opponents seize on the action and use it to stage an attack by accusation or question: the Judeans criticize the behavior of the healed man who is carrying his mat on the Sabbath (John 5:10–13). Third, the dominical reply to the attack, which is brief and compact, comes at the end: Jesus provides a rationale for the necessity of the healing miracle in terms of a continuation of divine work in human history (John 5:17).[19] Because the healing takes place on the Sabbath, Gerd Theissen classifies John 5:1–18 as one of "*justificatory rule miracles*,"[20] in which helping others prevails even over the sacred day of the Sabbath.

18. See Bultmann, *History of the Synoptic Tradition*, 39–45.

19. See further Borgen, *Early Christianity and Hellenistic Judaism*, 106–10; Asiedu-Peprah, *Johannine Sabbath Conflicts*, 16–19.

20. Theissen, *Miracle Stories*, 106 (italics original).

As to the structure, the unit of the healing-on-the-Sabbath contro-versy pericope has six scenes: (1) introduction and description (John 5:1–3), (2) prehealing encounter (John 5:5–7), (3) action and immediacy of healing (John 5:8–9), (4) judicial interrogation (John 5:10–13), (5) posthealing encounter (John 5:14–15), and (6) intensified overt persecu-tion (John 5:16–18).

## Narrative Analysis

### Introduction and Description (John 5:1–3)

The Johannine formula μετὰ ταῦτα (*meta tauta*, "after these things," John 5:1; see also 3:22; 5:14; 6:1; 7:1; 19:38) is employed as a literary device to signal the transition to a new section, which takes place in a differ-ent geographical setting from the previous event at Cana of Galilee (John 4:43–54). Jesus now travels to Jerusalem alone to attend ἑορτὴ τῶν Ἰουδαίων (*heortē tōn Ioudaiōn*, "a feast of the Judeans," John 5:1). Accord-ing to John's Gospel, this is the second of at least five visits to Jerusalem to celebrate Jewish feasts such as *Pesach*/Passover (John 2:13), "a feast of the Judeans" (John 5:1), *Sukkot*/Booths/Tabernacles (John 7:2), *Hanukkah*/Dedication (John 10:22), and *Pesach*/Passover (John 11:55; 12:1), thus underscoring the importance of Jerusalem as the religious and cultural center of Judaism in Jesus' time. Note that the evangelist purposely identi-fies all feasts except the one in John 5:1.

Certain manuscripts, such as P66, P75, A, and B, have the feminine noun ἑορτὴ (*heortē*, "feast," "celebration," "festival," John 5:1[21]) without the feminine definite article, whereas others, such as א and C, have it preceded by the feminine definite article ἡ (*hē*, "the"). Undoubtedly, the anarthrous reading seems certainly the most authentic interpretation since a scribal insertion of the feminine definite article would have meant to designate the unnamed feast in John 5:1 as either *Pesach*/Passover (John 6:4) or *Sukkot*/Booths/Tabernacles (John 7:2).[22] However, attempts have been made to identify the Johannine reference to the unspecified feast with one of the three pilgrimage festivals, known in Hebrew as שָׁלֹושׁ רְגָלִים (*Šālôš rĕgālîm*, "three legs," Exod 23:14–16; Deut 16:16), which are: פֶּסַח (*pesaḥ*, "Passover," Exod

---

21. See *BDAG*, 355.

22. See Barrett, *Gospel According to St. John*, 250–51; Brown, *Gospel According to John (I–XII)*, 206; Metzger, *Textual Commentary*, 207.

34:25[23]),[24] שָׁבֻעֹת (Šābuʿōt, "Weeks," "Pentecost," Exod 34:22[25]),[26] and סֻכּוֹת (sukkôt, "Booths," "Tabernacles," Deut 16:13[27]).[28] As a matter of fact, every Jewish male was required to travel to Jerusalem to celebrate the three pilgrimage festivals (Exod 23:17; Deut 16:16; Ant. 4.8.7 §203). At any rate, the nature, character, and identity of the innominate feast remain obscure.[29] One could correctly say that the evangelist probably uses the nameless feast as an opportunity to just bring Jesus back from Galilee to Jerusalem.

There is a textual problem with the Greek construction of John 5:2. The phrase, ἔστιν δὲ ἐν τοῖς Ἱεροσολύμοις ἐπὶ τῇ προβατικῇ κολυμβήθρα (estin de en tois Hierosolymois epi tē probatikē kolymbēthra), can be literally translated in two different ways. In both cases an English word is provided to elucidate its meaning. The key word seems to be κολυμβήθρα (kolymbēthra, "pool," "swimming-pool"[30]). If it is taken as nominative, then the noun ("gate") is supplied (". . . there is now in Jerusalem by the sheep gate a pool . . .").[31] However, if it is taken as dative, then the noun ("place") is inserted (". . . there is now in Jerusalem by the sheep pool, a place . . .").[32] The KJV supplies the noun ["market"] ("Now there is at Jerusalem by the sheep market a pool"). The nominative reading may offer a more satisfactory resolution on the basis of the reference to ἡ πύλη ἡ προβατική (hē pylē hē probatikē, "the gate of the sheep") in Nehemiah 3:1, 32; 12:39. This gate was near the north side of the Jerusalem Temple.

Prior to its archaeological discovery in the late nineteenth century, the pool of Bethesda, with its five colonnades (John 5:2), was thought to be an invention of the evangelist's imagination and, thus, the historicity of the pericope of the healing of the lame man was doubted. In the fifth century CE, Augustine, for example, presented an allegorical interpretation for it.

23. See BDB, 820.

24. See Bultmann, Gospel of John, 240.

25. See BDB, 988–89.

26. See Schnackenburg, Gospel According to St. John, 2:93; Beutler, Commentary on the Gospel of John, 147.

27. See BDB, 697.

28. See Köstenberger, John, 177.

29. See Carson, Gospel According to John, 241; Borchert, John 1–11, 230; Ridderbos, Gospel of John, 184.

30. See BDAG, 557.

31. See Bultmann, Gospel of John, 240; Carson, Gospel According to John, 241; NRSV.

32. See Brown, Gospel According to John (I–XII), 207; Schnackenburg, Gospel According to St. John, 2:94; Moloney, Gospel of John, 171.

In his opinion, the five colonnades of the pool of Bethesda symbolized the five books of Moses, which prescribed the law that did not bring acquittal to sinners, as the water of the pool of Bethesda did not bring healing to the multitudes of sick people (*Tract. Ev. Jo. 17.2*). However, archaeologists unearthed a massive structure of two adjacent pools separated by a wall, located in the courtyard of present-day St. Anne's Church in the Muslim Quarter of Jerusalem, confirming that the evangelist's description of the pool actually reflected accurate knowledge of Jerusalem.[33] The southern part of the pool was probably a large *mikveh*, viz., Jewish ritual bath, while the northern part was an *otzer*, viz., a reservoir feeding the *mikveh* with water. This may explain the stirring up of water in John 5:7. No information has been given as to the transference of the *mikveh-otzer* pool into a cultic healing sanctuary, which attracted many people with physical disability, deformity, and impairment, including the "blind, lame, and withered" (John 5:3). There is archaeological evidence confirming that the pool of Bethesda became in the second century CE a pagan site dedicated to the widespread cult of Asclepius, a Greek mythological god known for his healing power. Could this have been the reality during the time of Jesus? If so, then, the evangelist unmistakably presents Jesus "in competition with ancient healing sanctuaries."[34]

*Prehealing Encounter (John 5:5–7)*

One of the sick people lying at the pool of Bethesda is an anonymous minor character whose infirmity is unspecified. However, given Jesus' miracle-working command in John 5:8, the condition of this male character is more likely to be lameness than blindness. Lameness, as a physical disability, deformity, and impairment, causes its victims to be socially ostracized and religiously excluded from entering the Jerusalem Temple, as well as the assembly of God in the Qumranite community (Lev 21:16–20; 2 Sam 5:8; 1QSa 2:5–10). It is no surprise, then, that as an outcast, this lame man is frequently brought to the pool of Bethesda, hoping to be restored and healed, presumably by the therapeutic properties and qualities of its waters (John 5:7). He has been infirm "for thirty-eight years" (John 5:5). The length of his infirmity is a characteristic feature of healing-miracle stories

33. See Wahlde, "Archaeology and John's Gospel," 566; Murphy-O'Connor, *Holy Land*, 29–34; Burge, "Siloam, Bethesda, and the Johannine Water Motif," 3:261–62.

34. Theissen, *Miracle Stories*, 51.

(Mark 5:25; Luke 13:11; John 9:1; Acts 3:2). It is not meant to be taken symbolically or allegorically as an allusion pointing to the thirty-eight-year journey of the Israelites from Kadesh-barnea until the crossing of the Wadi Zered (Deut 2:14), but rather literally underlining the hopelessness and irremediability of the illness, and heightening at the same time the magnitude and actuality of the miracle to follow.[35]

The evangelist does not furnish information about why Jesus is at the pool of Bethesda. However, while there, he sees the lame man lying around the pool. He knows that he has been there for a long time. His knowledge is not natural, viz., acquired through inference based on observable evidence, but rather supernatural since it points to his extraordinary depth of knowledge of people (John 1:48; 2:25; 4:18; 13:38). Seizing the initiative in reaching out to the lame man, Jesus cuts right to the chase and speaks his first words, which naturally take the form of a straightforward question, Θέλεις ὑγιὴς γενέσθαι (*Theleis hygiēs genesthai*, "Do you desire to become healthy?," John 5:6). In the healing-miracle stories of the Gospels, individuals typically seek Jesus out to either heal them or cure their loved ones (e.g., Matt 8:5–6 || Luke 7:2–3; Mark 2:4; Luke 17:12–13; John 4:47). The present pericope is one of the few exceptions to this rule (e.g., Mark 3:1–3; Luke 13:12–13; 14:4; John 9:6). It should be clearly stated that the first words of the Johannine Jesus are not "entirely redundant in light of the man's obvious need,"[36] but rather meant to establish personal contact with the lame man and, consequently, create a vital space for dialogue (Mark 10:51; John 4:7). The Johannine adjective ὑγιὴς (*hygiēs*, "healthy," "sound"[37]) appears five times in the pericope (John 5:6, 9, 11, 14, 15; see also John 5:4; 7:23). Interestingly, it does not only refer to physical restoration of the lame man, but also includes socioreligious repair and restoration of his broken humanity.[38] The usage of ὑγιὴς (*hygiēs*) in John 5:6 recalls Mark 5:34, where Jesus commands the now-healed woman to be healthy from her disease.

The response of the lame man in John 5:7 reveals his lack of knowledge of who Jesus is and, consequently, shows his misunderstanding of Jesus' question. He respectfully calls him Κύριε (*Kyrie*, "Sir," "master," "lord,"

---

35. See, for example, Barrett, *Gospel According to St. John*, 253; Brown, *Gospel According to John (I–XII)*, 207; Schnackenburg, *Gospel According to St. John*, 2:95; Michaels, *Gospel of John*, 291; Keener, *Gospel of John*, 1:640.

36. Köstenberger, *John*, 180.

37. See *BDAG*, 1023.

38. See Kok, *New Perspectives*, 117.

"Lord," John 5:7), makes excuses for himself by stating that he has no man to put him into the pool when the water is bubbling, and acknowledges his inability to succeed in reaching the water of the pool first before anyone else does. He is convinced that the water of the pool has therapeutic properties and qualities. "He knows only one possibility," notes Ernst Haenchen, "viz., the healing powers of the pool."[39] Undoubtedly, the lame man's reply, which is based on popular belief in magic and superstition, is utterly fallacious at its core because it lacks empirical evidence.

### Action and Immediacy of Healing (John 5:8–9)

In response to the lame man's misunderstanding of his question, Jesus acts without hesitation or reservation. Thus, instead of lending a helping hand to him, Jesus intentionally utters the miracle-working command, Ἔγειρε ἆρον τὸν κράβαττόν σου καὶ περιπάτει (Egeire aron ton krabatton sou kai peripatei, "Arise, take up your mat and walk," John 5:8). The evangelist gives no explanation of why Jesus singles out this lame man to heal. It might be because he is the one who seems most in need among the blind, lame, and withered people around the pool. It is fascinating to note that this lame man neither displays trusting faith in Jesus nor requests healing from him, whether directly or indirectly. At any rate, Jesus' life-changing command is totally antithetical to the lame man's expectation and conviction. The only way out right now of his thirty-eight years of wretched misery and suffering is not to hold onto his hopeless belief in magic and superstition, but rather obey Jesus' liberating command. Interestingly, Jesus' miracle-working command is identical to the command spoken to the paralytic man in Capernaum, a town in Galilee (Mark 2:9). The Greek word κράβαττος (krabattos, John 5:8, 9, 10, 11; Mark 2:4, 9, 11, 12; 6:55; Acts 5:15; 9:33[40]) was a colloquial expression for a poor man's pallet or mattress.[41]

The evangelist uses εὐθέως (eutheōs, "immediately," "at once," John 5:9[42]) to show that the physical healing of the lame man is successful, instantaneous, complete, and absolute. The lame man carries out Jesus' command: he becomes healthy, takes up his mat, and walks away. The juxtaposition of the immediacy of the healing to the thirty-eight years of hopeless waiting is

39. Haenchen, John 1, 245.

40. See BDAG, 563.

41. See Brown, Gospel According to John (I–XII), 207–8.

42. See BDAG, 405.

striking. Jesus' mere command, not the water of the pool, has restored the lame man to health. Jesus, as the incarnate, divine Logos, Son, and Savior (John 1:14, 18; 3:16–17; 4:42), is God's ultimate representative on earth, exercising unlimited power over the natural world. He changes water into wine (John 2:1–12), heals sick people (John 4:43–54; 5:1–16; 9:1–39), multiplies five barley loaves and two fish to feed 5,000 people (John 6:1–14), walks on water (John 6:16–21), and raises a dead man (John 11:1–44).

The evangelist informs his audience that this transformative moment takes place on the Sabbath. John's Gospel reports two Sabbath-healing miracles (John 5:1–18; 9:1–39). On this point, it is in agreement with the Synoptic Gospels in relating that Jesus performs healing miracles on many Sabbaths (Mark 1:21–28, 29–31; 3:1–6; 6:1–6; Luke 13:10–17; 14:1–6). However, the Johannine reference to the Sabbath is quite different from the Synoptic Gospels. In contrast to the Synoptics (Mark 1:21; 3:2; 6:2; Luke 13:10; 14:1), John introduces the Sabbath after, and not before, Jesus' visible act of healing (John 5:9; 9:14). Some scholars regard the Sabbath motif as an integral, organic part of the original pericope,[43] while others consider it as secondary and, presumably and artificially, inserted by the evangelist into the pericope to provide an occasion for the controversy with the Judeans.[44] That the Sabbath forms a constituent part of the pericope is obvious from John 7:19–23. Raymond E. Brown correctly remarks, "One almost needs the Sabbath motif to give this story significance."[45]

*Judicial Interrogation (John 5:10–13)*

A phalanx of the Judeans, who are the guardians of the law, suddenly enters the scene. They raise harsh criticism against the behavior of the newly healed man, saying, Σάββατόν ἐστιν, καὶ οὐκ ἔξεστίν σοι ἆραι τὸν κράβαττον σου (*Sabbaton estin, kai ouk exestin soi arai ton krabatton sou*, "It is Sabbath, and it is unlawful for you to take up your mat," John 5:10). In Judaism, the Sabbath is set apart as a day of holiness and respite (Exod 20:8–11;

---

43. See Barrett, *Gospel According to St. John*, 254; Brown, *Gospel According to John (I–XII)*, 210; Beutler, *Commentary on the Gospel of John*, 149; Weiss, "Sabbath in the Fourth Gospel," 312–13; Ridderbos, *Gospel of John*, 186–87.

44. See Bultmann, *Gospel of John*, 239, 242; Dodd, *Historical Tradition*, 178–79; Schnackenburg, *Gospel According to St. John*, 2:92–93; Haenchen, *John 1*, 246, 255; Meier, *Marginal Jew*, 2:681.

45. Brown, *Gospel According to John (I–XII)*, 210.

31:12–17; 35:1–3; Deut 5:12–15; *J. W.* 2.17.10 §456). The Decalogue's fourth word clearly prohibits work on the Sabbath (cf. *Ant.* 3.5.5 §91). The Hebrew Bible prescribes the death penalty for a Sabbath violator (Exod 31:12–17; Deut 15:32–36). However, the question of what constitutes work had to be defined in Judaism to protect the sanctity of the Sabbath. The late seventh-/ early sixth-century-BCE prophet Jeremiah reminded the Israelites not to carry burdens on the Sabbath (Jer 17:21–22). Under the leadership of the mid-fifth-century-BCE Jewish governor Nehemiah, the gates of Jerusalem were closed to ensure no burden is brought into the city on the holy day of the Sabbath (Neh 13:15–22). Furthermore, carrying objects from one domain to another is one of the thirty-nine categories of work forbidden by the Mishnah on the Sabbath (*m. Šabb.*7:2).

The Judeans are shortsighted and narrow-minded; their attention focuses only on the apparent transgression of the Sabbath. They see the action of mat-carrying as a direct violation of the Sabbath. The now-healed man, therefore, stands accused of flaunting their understanding of the Sabbath observance. However, his alacritous response, Ὁ ποιήσας με ὑγιῆ ἐκεῖνός μοι εἶπεν, Ἆρον τὸν κράββατον σου καὶ περιπάτει (*Ho poiēsas me hygiē ekeinos moi eipen, Aron ton krabatton sou kai peripatei*, "The [one] having made me healthy, that one said to me, 'Take up your mat and walk,'" John 5:11), shows no accountability or culpability. It is evident that he justifies his behavior by explicitly stating that he is merely following an order of the miracle-worker who has made him healthy. Yet, his tone implicitly shifts the blame to Jesus. The Judeans are obviously not concerned with the disabled man's miraculous healing and restoration, but rather with the identity of the man who has enabled him to breach the Sabbath, Τίς ἐστιν ὁ ἄνθρωπος ὁ εἰπών σοι, Ἆρον καὶ περιπάτει (*Tis estin ho anthrōpos ho eipōn soi, Aron kai peripatei*, "Who is the man having said to you, 'Take up and walk?,'" John 5:12). This question is left hanging in the air unanswered due to the healed man's ignorance of the identity of the one who has made him healthy. The healing miracle itself has already begun to fade away from the scene. Note that the evangelist chooses to employ a narrative aside, ὁ γὰρ Ἰησοῦς ἐξένευσεν ὄχλου ὄντος ἐν τῷ τόπῳ (*ho gar Iēsous exeneusen ochlou ontos en tō topō*, "for Jesus withdrew, a crowd being in the place," John 5:13), to explain what Jesus does after healing the lame man.

## Posthealing Encounter (John 5:14–15)

It is evident that the Johannine formula μετὰ ταῦτα (*meta tauta*, "after these things," John 5:14) signals a change of time and place in the narrative. A considerable length of time must have passed between Jesus' miraculous healing of the lame man at the pool of Bethesda and Jesus' finding him, whether intentionally or accidentally, in Jerusalem Temple. It is also obvious that the effect of Jesus' miraculous healing of the lame man extends beyond the perimeter of physical restoration to encompass full socioreligious integration and immersion in the life and culture of the Jewish community in Jerusalem.

Throughout the pericope, Jesus is in complete control: he sees the lame man at the pool of Bethesda (John 5:6); he initiates a conversation with him (John 5:6); he heals him (John 5:8); and now he finds him in the Jerusalem Temple (John 5:14), "the place of the presence of God on earth,"[46] probably praying and offering sacrifices to God. Jesus speaks to him and reminds him of the permanent state of his physical healing, Ἴδε ὑγιὴς γέγονας (*Ide hygiēs gegonas*, "Look! You have become healthy," John 5:14). God's gift of new life (cf. John 7:23), bestowed upon the now-healed man through Jesus, needs to be nurtured by avoiding sin. For this reason, Jesus explicitly warns him, μηκέτι ἁμάρτανε, ἵνα μὴ χεῖρόν σοί τι γένηται (*mēketi hamartane, hina mē cheiron soi ti genētai*, "sin no more, lest something worse may happen to you," John 5:14). One can rightly extrapolate from this saying of the Johannine Jesus that there is a causal connection between personal sin and physical sickness. Sin, in John's Gospel, is the failure to come to believe in Jesus, who is God's ultimate revealer sent from above (John 3:13, 31; 6:33, 38; 8:23–24) to provide access to eternal life (John 3:15; 4:14; 5:24; 6:40; 10:10; 11:25–26; 17:1–3). In contrast to the Samaritan woman (John 4:39), the royal official man (John 4:53), and the blind man (John 9:38), this now-healed man does not come to faith. He fails to move from ignorance to knowledge. As R. Alan Culpepper notes, "The healing of the man at the pool of Bethesda fails to produce an *anagnorisis*."[47] Gerald O'Collins does not hesitate to assert that, "Meeting Jesus and even being physically healed by him does not irresistibly rouse faith and transform a human life."[48]

---

46. Jeremias, *Jerusalem in the Time of Jesus*, 75.

47. Culpepper, *Gospel and Letters of John*, 80.

48. O'Collins, *Rethinking Fundamental Theology*, 187–88.

The healed man absolutely ignores Jesus' admonition. He goes back to the Judeans and notifies them that the miracle-worker who has made him healthy is none other than Jesus himself (John 5:15). Thus, the Judeans' question, left hanging in mid-air (John 5:12), is completely answered. It is difficult, if not impossible, to explain the puzzling, if not shocking, behavior of the healed man. Why does he behave in such a manner? What is his motive? The verb ἀναγγέλλειν (*anangellein*, John 5:15[49]) has two totally different meanings. It can mean "to report information back." Therefore, most Johannine scholars interpret the behavior of the healed man negatively: he becomes an informant and a betrayer.[50] However, the verb can also mean "to announce" and "to proclaim." Thus, Gail R. O'Day and Susan Hylen do not view him as a traitor, but rather as a proclaimer who announces to the Judeans "the good news of his healer's identity."[51]

### Intensified Overt Persecution (John 5:16–18)

Either way, the healed man's behavior ultimately brings the Judeans in direct contact with Jesus, leading to ever-deepening controversy in the Jerusalem Temple. It becomes apparent that the Judeans are convinced that Jesus' miraculous healing of the lame man on the Sabbath is an act of contravention, which needs not be tolerated. Therefore, they publicly resort to continually mistreating him (διώκειν, *diōkein*, "to persecute," John 5:16[52]). Their demeanor constitutes the first open display of bellicosity toward Jesus in John's Gospel.

Becoming cognizant of their mistreatment, Jesus utters a theological pronouncement, Ὁ πατήρ μου ἕως ἄρτι ἐργάζεται κἀγὼ ἐργάζομαι (*Ho patēr mou heōs arti ergazetai kagō ergazomai*, "My father is [still] working until now, and I [too] am working," John 5:17). It is significant to point out that, throughout John's Gospel, Jesus calls God, the creator of the universe, ὁ πατήρ μου (*ho patēr mou*, "my father," John 2:16; 5:43; 6:32; 8:19; 10:18; 14:2; 15:1; 20:17). He is relationally, intimately, and exclusively dependent on, not independent from, God. As God's only begotten Son (μονογενής,

---

49. See *BDAG*, 59.

50. See, for example, Barrett, *Gospel According to St. John*, 255; Schnackenburg, *Gospel According to St. John*, 2:98; Keener, *Gospel of John*, 1:644; Michaels, *Gospel of John*, 299.

51. O'Day and Hylen, *John*, 65.

52. See *BDAG*, 254.

*monogenēs*, "one and only," "unique," John 1:14, 18; 3:16, 18[53]), Jesus does what God the Father does (John 5:19). His miraculous healing of the lame man at the pool of Bethesda on the Sabbath is, therefore, in continuation with God's creative and restorative work in the universe.

There is no doubt that the priestly author of the first creation narrative in Genesis 1:1—2:4a explicitly affirms that God rested (שָׁבַת, *Šābat*, "to rest," "to desist from labor"[54]) on the seventh day from all the work of creation (Gen 2:2–3). Yet, despite such affirmation, it is illogical to think that God is inactive in human history. For example, Philo of Alexandria, a first-century-CE Jewish philosopher and a contemporary of Jesus, states that God never desists from creating and working (*Alleg. Interp.* 1:5–6; *Cherubim* 87). In principle, then, Jesus does not transgress the Sabbath, but rather disagrees with the Judeans' legalistic interpretation that a Sabbath violation has in fact taken place. The evangelist writes that the Judeans understand Jesus' theological pronouncement in John 5:17 as a claim to equality with God: ἴσον ἑαυτὸν ποιῶν τῷ Θεῷ (*ison heauton poiōn tō Theō*, "making himself equal to God," John 5:18). The controversy swiftly shifts from Jesus being accused of violating the Sabbath to Jesus being accused of blasphemy. Consequently, the level of bellicosity aimed by the Judeans toward Jesus escalates from an overt mistreatment to now seeking to kill him (John 5:18). This is the first reference in John's Gospel to the Judeans' plan to eliminate Jesus (John 7:1, 19, 20, 25; 8:37, 40; 11:53). The Johannine reference to killing Jesus recalls the plot of the Pharisees and the Herodians to put Jesus to death after his healing of the man with a withered hand on the Sabbath (Mark 3:1–6). In both Gospels, Jesus is seen as a threat to religiopolitical authorities and leaders.

---

53. See *BDAG*, 658.
54. See *BDB*, 991–92.

# 7

# "Woman, Where Are They?"

## Text

53 Then each of them went home, 1 while Jesus went to the Mount of Olives. 2 Early in the morning he came again to the temple. All the people came to him and he sat down and began to teach them. 3 The scribes and the Pharisees brought a woman who had been caught in adultery; and making her stand before all of them, 4 they said to him, "Teacher, this woman was caught in the very act of committing adultery. 5 Now in the law Moses commanded us to stone such women. Now what do you say?" 6 They said this to test him, so that they might have some charge to bring against him. Jesus bent down and wrote with his finger on the ground. 7 When they kept on questioning him, he straightened up and said to them, "Let anyone among you who is without sin be the first to throw a stone at her." 8 And once again he bent down and wrote on the ground. 9 When they heard it, they went away, one by one, beginning with the elders; and Jesus was left alone with the woman standing before him. 10 Jesus straightened up and said to her, "Woman, where are they? Has no one condemned you?" 11 She said, "No one, sir." And Jesus said, "Neither do I condemn you. Go your way, and from now on do not sin again."

John 7:53—8:11 (NRSV)[1]

## Scholarly Context

THE PERICOPE OF THE adulterous woman (John 7:53—8:11), traditionally nestled between John 7:52 and John 8:12 in the great majority of manuscripts, is perhaps one of the best-known and most popular stories of John's

1. The pericope of John 7:53—8:11, or John 8:1–11, is liturgically read on the fifth Sunday of Lent, Cycle C.

Gospel. It has long been the subject of intense scholarly interest and debate since its inception. There exists nearly virtual unanimity among Johannine scholars today that this pericope is a later non-Johannine interpolation added to the original text of John's Gospel.[2] John P. Heil has attempted, albeit unsuccessfully, to challenge this scholarly consensus by arguing that the internal linguistic and thematic literary links of the present pericope point to Johannine authenticity.[3] Daniel B. Wallace has offered a rebuttal against such an argument, thus defending the scholarly position that the present pericope did not originally form part of John's Gospel.[4] The NRSV, for example, encloses John 7:53—8:11 with double square brackets, and includes a note about its debatable textual authenticity and variations.

The external and internal evidence, in fact, substantially and overwhelmingly leave no doubt that the pericope of the adulterous woman was not an authentic part of John's Gospel. First, the pericope has a peculiar and problematic textual history. It is completely absent, as Bruce M. Metzger points out, from the very oldest, extant Greek papyri and uncial codices, such as P66, P75, ℵ, A, B, C, W (ca. 400-450 CE), as well as from the earliest versions of Old Syriac, Coptic, Latin, Armenian, and Georgian manuscripts, ranging from the third to the fifth century CE.[5] However, the most conspicuous two anomalies are Jerome's Latin Vulgate and the Greek-Latin bilingual D.

Patristic writers and commentators oscillate between extreme silence about and explicit reference to John 7:53—8:11. On the one hand, Tatian (ca. 120-180 CE), Irenaeus (ca. 130-202 CE), Tertullian (ca. 155-240 CE), Origen (ca. 184-253 CE), Aphrahat (ca. 285-345 CE), Ephrem (ca. 306-373 CE), Theodore of Mopsuestia (ca. 350-428 CE), and Cyril of Alexandria (ca. 376-444 CE) make no mention of it. On the other hand, the early third-century-CE anonymous author of *Didascalia Apostolorum* (*Did. apost.* 7.2:24), Didymus the Blind (ca. 313-398 CE; *Comm. Eccl.* 233.7-13), Pacian of Barcelona (ca. 310-391 CE; *Ep. III* 3.20.1), Ambrose of Milan (ca. 339-397 CE; *Ep. XXV* 4-7; *Ep. XXVI* 2), Rufinus (ca. 334-411 CE; *Apol.*

---

2. See Lightfoot, *St. John's Gospel*, 345; Brown, *Gospel According to John (I-XII)*, 335; Barrett, *Gospel According to St. John*, 589; Schnackenburg, *Gospel According to St. John*, 2:162; Ridderbos, *Gospel of John*, 285, Moloney, *Gospel of John*, 259; Keener, *Gospel of John*, 1:735; Haenchen, *John 1*, 46.

3. See Heil, "Story of Jesus and the Adulteress," 182-91.

4. See Wallace, "Reconsidering," 290-96.

5. See Metzger, *Textual Commentary*, 219-20; cf. Metzger and Ehrman, *Text of the New Testament*, 319-21; GNT, 347.

*Hier* 1.44), Jerome (ca. 347–420 CE; *Pelag* 2:17), and Augustine (ca. 345–430 CE; *Incomp. nupt.* 2:6–7; *Tract. Ev. Jo.* 33), allude to it either partially or entirely. The reference of Papias (ca. 60–130 CE), bishop of Hierapolis, to a story of a woman accused of many sins before the Lord (Eusebius, *Hist. eccl.* 3.39.17) cannot be an allusion to John 7:53—8:11 because the woman in it is accused of many unidentified sins, while John 7:53—8:11 speaks only of one single sin of adultery. Furthermore, Eusebius relates that Papias's reference can be found in the Gospel of the Hebrews, not John's. It seems that Papias's reference is much closer to the story of the sinful woman whose many sins were pronounced forgiven by Jesus (cf. Luke 7:36–50).[6]

Second, the positioning of the pericope shows some fluidity. It is found, in addition to its traditional location between John 7:52 and John 8:12, placed in other alternative locations, about a dozen in number, in certain late manuscripts of John's Gospel as well as Luke's.[7] It may suffice to mention that the twelfth-/thirteenth-century-CE minuscule manuscript families, designated *f*1 and *f*13, have it positioned after John 21:25 and Luke 21:38, respectively. This may indicate that this pericope was originally an independent and free-floating written story about Jesus, inserted by scribes, perhaps during the third century CE between John 7:52 and John 8:12. Although it awkwardly seems to break up and interrupt the unity of the flow of Jesus' discourse in John 7:1–52 and John 8:12–59,[8] it was not, as Luke T. Johnson incorrectly suggests, "so mechanically placed in its present location,"[9] but rather, writes Rudolf Schnackenburg, "it was certainly not done without considerable thought."[10] As a matter of fact, the pericope accentuates certain themes in John 7:1–52 and John 8:12–59, such as teaching in the temple (John 7:14, 28; 8:2, 20), interpreting the law (John 7:19, 51; 8:5, 17), and judging and condemning (John 7:24, 51; 8:11, 15, 26).[11]

Third, although the pericope contains some apparent Johannine features, such as the expression μηκέτι ἁμάρτανε (*mēketi hamartane*, "sin

6. See Petersen, "ΟΥΔΕ ΕΓΩ ΣΕ [ΚΑΤΑ]ΚΡΙΝΩ," 196–98; Edwards, *Hebrew Gospel*, 7–10.

7. See Keith, *Pericope Adulterae*, 119–21.

8. See Lightfoot, *St. John's Gospel*, 346; Witherington, *John's Wisdom*, 164; Ridderbos, *Gospel of John*, 285; Beutler, *Commentary on the Gospel of John*, 226–27.

9. Johnson, *Writings of the New Testament*, 544–45.

10. Schnackenburg, *Gospel According to St. John*, 2:171.

11. See Lightfoot, *St. John's Gospel*, 347; Brown, *Gospel According to John (I–XII)*, 336; Maccini, *Her Testimony Is True*, 234; O'Day and Hylen, *John*, 89; Heil, "Story of Jesus and the Adulteress," 185–90.

no more," John 8:11; see also John 5:14) and the narrative aside τοῦτο δὲ ἔλεγον πειράζοντες αὐτόν (*touto de elegon peirazontes auton*, "now they were saying this testing him" John 8:6a; see also John 6:6a),[12] it is more Synoptic than Johannine in style and vocabulary. It most closely resembles the controversy stories found in the Synoptic Gospels (e.g., Matt 22:15–22 ‖ Mark 12:13–17 ‖ Luke 20:20–26); though Jesus' climatic rebuttal is different in John 7:53—8:11. Strikingly enough, it echoes Luke's style (Luke 19:47; 21:37–38; 22:39).[13] Certain vocabulary words and expressions, such as Ὄρος τῶν Ἐλαιῶν (*Oros tōn Elaiōn*, "Mount of Olives," John 8:1), Ὄρθρου (*Orthrou*, "at daybreak," John 8:2), παρεγένετο (*paregeneto*, "he came," John 8:2), πᾶς ὁ λαὸς (*pas ho laos*, "all the people," John 8:2), καθίσας (*kathisas*, "having sat down," John 8:2), οἱ γραμματεῖς (*hoi grammateis*, "the scribes," John 8:3), and τῶν πρεσβυτέρων (*tōn presbyterōn*, "the elders," John 8:9) are mentioned nowhere else in John's Gospel, but have unique affinities with the Synoptists.

It is interesting to see how some Johannine scholars still remain divided over the questions pertaining to the pericope's historicity, canonicity, and homiletics. Rudolf Bultmann, who classifies John 7:53—8:11 as an apocryphal apophthegm,[14] does not cover it in his commentary on John's Gospel. Andreas J. Köstenberger states that "proper conservatism and caution suggest that the passage be omitted from preaching in the churches (not to mention inclusion in the main body of translations, even within square brackets)."[15] Conversely, Gerald L. Borchert writes, "For most in the Church, Protestants (including the present writer) and Roman Catholics alike, this pericope is regarded as being fully canonical."[16] At any rate, just because the Johannine authorship of John 7:53—8:11 is dubious, it does not mean that the pericope's historicity, canonicity, and homiletics should be discriminated against. It is evident that this pericope is not an imaginary tale invented by a scribe, but rather a historical account of great antiquity, genuinely belonging to the first-century historical Jesus himself.[17] For

---

12. See Punch, "Piously Offensive Pericope Adulterae," 18; Heil, "Story of Jesus and the Adulteress," 184–85.

13. See further Cadbury, "Possible Case of Lukan Authorship," 237–44.

14. See Bultmann, *History of the Synoptic Tradition*, 63.

15. Köstenberger, *John*, 248.

16. Borchert, *John 1–11*, 369.

17. See Brown, *Gospel According to John (I–XII)*, 333; Barrett, *Gospel According to St. John*, 590; Schnackenburg, *Gospel According to St. John*, 2:170; Moloney, *Gospel of John*, 262; Metzger, *Textual Commentary*, 220; Keener, *Gospel of John*, 1:736; Derrett, *Law in*

example, lapidation, as a common form of execution for a range of crimes, such as adultery, blasphemy, idolatry, and sorcery, was still practiced in Jesus' time (Matt 21:35; Mark 10:2–12; Luke 20:6; John 8:59; 10:31; 11:8; Acts 7:58; 14:19; *Ant.* 20.9.1 §200). Furthermore, the portrait of Jesus, his intent and behavior, is coherent with the overall presentation of him found elsewhere in the Gospels, particularly his nonjudgmental attitude toward and acceptance of sinners, who were considered social and religious outcasts in first-century-CE Judaism (Mark 2:13–17; Luke 7:36–50; 15:11–31; 19:1–10; John 4:1–42). Finally, the vitriolic proclivity of some religious leaders to deliberately put a question to Jesus in order to test and challenge him on subjects pertaining to interpreting the Jewish law and politics is historically authentic. The verb πειράζειν (*peirazein*, "to put to test," "to tempt," John 8:6[18]) is found in most of the Synoptic controversy stories (e.g., Mark 8:11 || Matt 16:1 || Luke 11:16; Mark 10:2 || Matt 19:3; Mark 12:15 || Matt 22:18; Matt 22:35 || Luke 10:25). Though originally not part of John's Gospel, the Catholic Church, since the acceptance of Jerome's Latin Vulgate as its official authoritative translation of the Bible in the Council of Trent (1545–1563), has recognized the canonicity of John 7:53—8:11.

## Literary Genre and Structure

In terms of literary genre, the pericope does not fit neatly into any of the form-critical categories. It is probably a mixture of a biographical apophthegm and a controversy story. As a subcategory of Rudolf Bultmann's apophthegms, a biographical apophthegm focuses mainly on Jesus' saying, which is given in a concise manner and comes at the end of the pericope:[19] Jesus says to the adulterous woman, "Neither do I condemn you; go, [and] from now on sin no more" (John 8:11). This powerful saying, placed at the end of the pericope, "functions as a brilliant *coup de théâtre*."[20] As a controversy story, the pericope has some characteristic elements exhibiting a threefold pattern typical of rabbinic discussion.[21] First, the starting point lies in some action or attitude: some representatives of Jewish religious leaders, who are Jesus' main antagonists, appear on the scene, bringing

---

the New Testament, 156.

18. See *BDAG*, 792–93.

19. See Bultmann, *History of the Synoptic Tradition*, 55–56, 62, 63.

20. Petersen, "ΟΥΔΕ ΕΓΩ ΣΕ [ΚΑΤΑ]ΚΡΙΝΩ," 192.

21. See Bultmann, *History of the Synoptic Tradition*, 39–45.

a woman caught in adultery: "Now the scribes and the Pharisees bring a woman having been caught in adultery" (John 8:3). Second, the opponents seize this opportunity to stage an attack by accusation or question: some representatives of Jewish religious leaders publicly challenge Jesus with a direct question about a religiopolitical issue: "Now in the law Moses commanded us to stone [to death] such [women]. But you—what do you say?" (John 8:5). It is obvious that asking Jesus about his stance *vis-à-vis* the Mosaic law is intended to entrap him: "This now they were saying testing him so that they might have [something] to accuse him" (John 8:6). Third, Jesus' reply, which culminates in his ability to deflect his interlocutors' polemic question with a fitting riposte, inevitably leads to their public shame and humiliation: Jesus answers them with a saying which will eventually extricate him and the woman from the trap of his interlocutors, "The sinless among you let him first cast a stone at her" (John 8:7).

As to structure, the pericope consists of four scenes: (1) introduction and description (John 7:53—8:2), (2) statement of case and challenge (John 8:3–6a), (3) riposte to the challenge (John 8:6b–9a), and (4) verdict (John 8:9b–11).

## Narrative Analysis

### Introduction and Description (John 7:53—8:2)

In John's Gospel, Jesus goes up to Jerusalem to celebrate the feast of סֻכּוֹת (*sukkôt*, "Booths," "Tabernacles," John 7:10). He takes advantage of its joyous atmosphere to teach the pilgrims in the precincts of the Jerusalem Temple (John 7:14, 28, 37). This feast begins on the fifteenth day of Tishri (September-October) and is commemorated for eight days (Lev 23:33–36, 39–43; Num 29:12–39; Deut 16:13–15; *Ant.* 8.4.1 §100). During this time, Jewish people constructed temporary shelters, made from branches and leaves, and dwelt in them as a reminder of their ancestors, the Israelites, who lived in tents for forty years after their emancipation, under Moses' leadership, from slavery in Egypt.

Whatever peculiar and problematic textual history and placement of the pericope of the adulterous woman may have been, in its current Johannine context (John 7:53—8:11) it takes place in the precincts of the Jerusalem Temple where Jesus is teaching the day after the conclusion of the autumn harvest festival of סֻכּוֹת (sukkôt). John 7:53—8:2 lends strong credence to this point of view.

The phrase, Καὶ ἐπορεύθησαν ἕκαστος εἰς τὸν οἶκον αὐτοῦ (Kai eporeuthēsan hekastos eis ton oikon autou, "And they went each to his house," John 7:53), indicates that the last day of the feast of סֻכּוֹת (sukkôt) is over (John 7:37). The subject of ἐπορεύθησαν (eporeuthēsan, "they went") is unspecified. It can refer back to either the pilgrims who leave their constructed temporary shelters and go home after the last day of the festival (John 7:37–44), or to the chief priests and Pharisees who have a debate with Nicodemus over Jesus (John 7:45–52). Jesus, however, ἐπορεύθη εἰς τὸ Ὄρος τῶν Ἐλαιῶν (eporeuthē eis to Oros tōn Elaiōn, "went into the Mount of Olives," John 8:1), which is a ridge situated outside the city walls of Jerusalem to the east, to lodge there at night (cf. Luke 21:37). There is no mention as to whom Jesus stays with. Jerome Murphy-O'Connor points out that Jesus might have found accommodation with Martha, Mary, and Lazarus in Bethany (cf. John 11:1; Mark 11:11; Matt 21:17), which is on the eastern slope of the Mount of Olives.[22]

The next day, Jesus walks down the slope of the Mount of Olives, through the Kidron Valley, and comes up to the precincts of the Jerusalem Temple without his entourage, viz., the disciples. He unflinchingly picks up where he left off the previous day, despite having his life threatened by some of the crowd and the Temple guards who unsuccessfully attempt to arrest him during the feast of סֻכּוֹת (sukkôt, John 7:30, 32, 44, 45). Like a magnet, Jesus attracts early morning Temple visitors and worshippers to himself, καὶ πᾶς ὁ λαὸς ἤρχετο πρὸς αὐτόν (kai pas ho laos ērcheto pros auton, "and all the people were coming to him," John 8:2). The sight of all people coming to see Jesus prompts him to sit down, like rabbis of his day, and teach them. The posture of καθίσας (kathisas, "setting down," John 8:2; cf. Mark 9:35; Matt 5:1; Luke 5:3) "was the customary indication," writes Jacob Neusner, "that serious teaching was going to commence."[23] The narrator does not specify the content of Jesus' teaching. There is a linguistic link between John 8:2 and John 7:14. In both verses, the verb διδάσκειν (didaskein, "to teach," "to instruct"[24]) is used in the imperfect (ἐδίδασκεν, edidasken, "was teaching," "began to teach") to describe Jesus teaching the crowd in the precincts of the Jerusalem Temple. It is worth noting that the locale of Jesus' teaching is in

22. See Murphy-O'Connor, Keys to Jerusalem, 103.

23. Neusner, Rabbi Talks with Jesus, 21.

24. See BDAG, 241.

the treasury of the Jerusalem Temple (cf. John 8:20; Mark 12:41–44 || Luke 21:1–4), known also as the women's court because it was the only Temple court where Jewish women (and men) were permitted to enter and worship (*J.W.* 5.5.2 §199; *Ag. Ap.* 2.8 §§103–4). It is clear that John 8:2 provides a backdrop for what is about to ensue.

### Statement of Case and Challenge (John 8:3–6a)

The scribes and Pharisees (cf. Matt 23:13; Luke 5:21), who were members of the supreme judicial council of Judaism, viz., the Sanhedrin (*Ant.* 13.16.2 §408; 18.1.4 §17), burst into the women's court, bringing to Jesus an anonymous γυναῖκα ἐπὶ μοιχείᾳ κατειλημμένην (*gynaika epi moicheia kateilēmmenēn*, "woman having been caught in adultery," John 8:3). Adultery is a violation of the Decalogue's seventh word (Exod 20:14; Deut 5:18; *Ant.* 3.5.5 §92). It is viewed as a crime against one's property rights and an insult to one's honor. Thus, it occurs when a man has voluntary sexual intercourse with an engaged girl (Deut 22:23–24) or a married woman (Lev 18:20; 20:16, 20; Deut 22:22), whose body and sexuality, legally and exclusively, belong rather to the ownership of either her father, brother, or husband, respectively.

The verb καταλαμβάνειν (*katalambanein*, "to seize," "to catch"[25]) indicates that the woman has been apprehended by surprise, probably by at least two or three Jewish male witnesses (Num 35:30; Deut 17:6; 19:15) who must have broken into the private space and boundary of her house in Jerusalem, and found her intimately involved in sexual intercourse with a man other than her husband. Was she a victim of male sexual entrapment? Was she coerced into this forbidden sexual relationship? Was she voluntarily invested in this illicit sexual relationship because of feelings of salacious passion or numbing boredom? Did she take advantage of her husband's absence to engage in sexually inappropriate conduct with a complete stranger (cf. Prov 7:10–20)? Why was she the only one caught? What about her paramour in crime? Did he disappear into thin air? Did he manage to pay off the witnesses? Was he let go because he was a prominent figure? Although these lingering questions remain unanswered and unanswerable, one thing is for sure: the absence of the male paramour in crime is conducive to sexual double standard, viz., implementing stronger punishments for a woman's sexual expression and allowing men more

25. See *BDAG*, 519–20.

latitude in sexual conduct. At any rate, J. Duncan M. Derrett argues that the adulterous woman, who was actually seen *in coitu*, was certainly caught in a trap set up by her husband who became suspicious of her. He adds that the sin of both the husband and witnesses was that they failed in preventing the crime of adultery from being committed.[26]

The adulterous woman must have been dragged out of her house, probably half-clad, and brought to the scribes and Pharisees, probably to have her lynched by male witnesses as well as a zealous crowd. This collective barbaric behavior is a clear visible sign of androcentric violence and prejudice against women in first-century-Palestinian Judaism. Having brought the adulterous woman to Jesus, the scribes and Pharisees make a spectacle of her by having her stand, as a passive object, ἐν μέσῳ (*en mesō*, "in the middle," "in the midst," John 8:3) of all those gathered around Jesus to hear his teaching. "She is an object on display," writes Gail R. O'Day, "given no name, no voice, no identity apart from that for which she stands accused."[27] This married woman is publicly dehumanized, traumatized, and defenseless. Her nonnormative sexual act, as viewed by her accusers, threatens the fabric of their sociocultural Jewish identity. Adultery, as a proscribed sexual act, "strikes at the heart of the patriarchal social order."[28] She is consequently standing there, staring death in the face.

Jesus' space, on the other hand, is also invaded, violated, and his teaching to the people around him has been interrupted by the arrival of the scribes and Pharisees. He must have glanced up at them from his seated position. Significantly, they address him as Διδάσκαλε (*Didaskale*, "Teacher," John 8:4), thus shifting the account from narration to dialogue. At times, the Greek title διδάσκαλος (*didaskalos*, "teacher") is used alone (John 8:4; 11:28; 13:13–14), while at other times it is utilized to translate the Aramaic titles רַבִּי (*rabbî*) and רַבּוּנִי (*rabbônî*) in John 1:38 and 20:16, but never in John 1:49, 6:25, or 11:8. The scribes and Pharisees' use of διδάσκαλος (*didaskalos*) never coincides with a legitimate recognition of Jesus as an equal. As a matter of fact, the Pharisees, in collaboration with the chief priests, have earlier commissioned the Temple guards to arrest Jesus during the festival of סֻכּוֹת (*sukkôt*, John 7:32, 45–49). They will later call a meeting of the Sanhedrin to plan the arrest and death of Jesus (John 11:45–53, 57). At any rate, Jesus is aware of their crafty maneuver of deception and false flattery.

26. See Derrett, *Law in the New Testament*, 161–64.

27. O'Day, "John 7:53—8:11," 632.

28. Green, "Making her Case," 246.

The scribes and Pharisees proceed to state to Jesus the fact of the case against the adulterous woman, αὕτη ἡ γυνὴ κατείληπται ἐπ' αὐτοφώρῳ μοιχευομένη (hautē hē gynē kateilēptai ep' autophōrō moicheuomenē, "this woman has been caught in the very act of committing adultery," John 8:4). The derogatory attitude of the scribes and Pharisees toward the adulterous woman, who has been caught *in flagranti*,[29] is conspicuously repugnant. They use the female demonstrative pronoun αὕτη (hautē, "this"), which has a pejorative connotation, to refer to her. She is treated like a nobody. Not even once is she directly addressed by them. On the other hand, she, with her self-accusing silence, says or does nothing to protest against the cruel and ignominious treatment of the scribes and Pharisees, or even contradict the accusation raised against her.

The scribes and Pharisees put this menacing and polemic question to Jesus, ἐν δὲ τῷ νόμῳ ἡμῖν Μωϋσῆς ἐνετείλατο τὰς τοιαύτας λιθάζειν. σὺ οὖν τί λέγεις (en de tō nomō hēmin Mōusēs eneteilato tas toiautas lithazein. sy oun ti legeis, "in the law now Moses commanded us to stone [to death] such [women]; but you—what do you say?," John 8:5). It is quite obvious that the scribes and Pharisees are not seeking legal advice from Jesus on this particular case. There is some substantial evidence to back up this conclusion. First, they were known to be literate religious groups and regarded as Judaism's official legal experts, interpreters, and teachers of the Mosaic law and traditional customs. They knew exactly what the law meant and required. "As far as they were concerned," writes J. Ramsey Michaels, "there could be only one 'right' answer to their question: that the stoning should proceed as the law required."[30] Second, they were Jesus' main antagonists (cf. Mark 7:1; Matt 23:2; Luke 11:53). The narrator's narrative aside acknowledges that their intent is nefarious: "This now they were saying testing him so that they might have [something] to accuse him" (John 8:6a; cf. Luke 6:7). They are using this disarrayed woman as bait to publicly entrap and delegitimize Jesus in front of all the people, as well as the Sanhedrin. They think that their question has backed him into a corner. They know that the only way to solve this situation is through lynching, an act of an angry and violent mob. In fact, Jesus and his followers were no strangers to threats of lynching. Jesus himself narrowly escaped being lynched at least three times (Luke 4:29; John 8:59; 10:39). Stephen, a disciple and deacon in Jerusalem,

---

29. See Schnackenburg, *Gospel According to St. John*, 2:165; Moloney, *Gospel of John*, 260.

30. Michaels, *Gospel of John*, 496.

was murdered as the result of a mob-impassioned lynching (Acts 7:54–60). On his first journey, Paul survived lynching in Lystra (Acts 14:19; cf. 2 Cor 11:25). He was also rescued by the Roman tribune in Jerusalem from lynching (Acts 21:30–36). Lynching does not require legal trial or formal verdict by the Sanhedrin. There is a debate among scholars whether the Sanhedrin retained or lost its power to inflict capital punishment in Jesus' day. It seems that John 11:47–53, where the Sanhedrin is convened to plan to put Jesus to death, contradicts John 18:31, where the Sanhedrin acknowledges to Pilate it has no authority to carry out capital punishment. Some rabbinic statements, such as *'Abodah Zarah*, support John 18:31 (*b. 'Abod. Zar.* 8b).

### Riposte to the Challenge (John 8:6b–9a)

The question of the scribes and Pharisees regarding lapidation, the truth must be told, seems to force Jesus into a dilemma. On the one hand, if he prohibits it, he then would violate the Mosaic law, which unambiguously states that the crime of adultery is death for both the adulterer and the adulteress (Lev 20:10; Deut 22:22, 24; *Ant.* 3.12.1 §§274–75). He consequently would be vilified as a false Galilean teacher and prophet (cf. John 7:52), misleading people by his unorthodox attitude toward the obscene crime of adultery. Jesus must be careful not to flagrantly contradict Moses, a thirteenth-century-BCE figure, who is presented in the Hebrew Bible as a leader, miracle-worker, liberator, law-receiver, law-giver, judge, covenant-mediator, and transcriber of the Torah, thus making him the most prominent figure in Israel's religious and political affairs. On the other hand, if he permits it, he then would discredit his own liberating attitude and disposition towards women, as particularly seen in his encounter with the Samaritan woman where he does not condemn her because of her complicated marital history (John 4:16–18). Moreover, if he authorizes it, he then would directly infringe on the authority of the Roman procurator who has arrogated to himself the prerogative to adjudicate capital cases (*J.W.* 2.8.1 §117). Either answer renders Jesus a subject for religious (Sanhedrin) or political (Roman) excoriation.[31]

---

31. See Lightfoot, *St. John's Gospel*, 348; Barrett, *Gospel According to St. John*, 591–92; Brown, *Gospel According to John (I–XII)*, 337; Schnackenburg, *Gospel According to St. John*, 2:164; Witherington, *Women and the Genesis of Christianity*, 39; Kinukawa, "On John 7:53—8:11," 2:90; Derrett, *Law in the New Testament*, 170–71.

All this seems to leave Jesus, who is now standing facing the scribes and Pharisees, in a quandary. The only fact presented to him is that this anonymous married woman has been caught in the very act of sexual intercourse with a man other than her husband. What is lacking from this case, however, is the presence of her husband and two or three reliable witnesses, who are nowhere to be found, to testify against her and be the first to carry out the execution if she is convicted. What is also missing is the woman's partner in crime. This case is unmistakably in violation of the Mosaic law.

Thus, rather than answering their question directly, Jesus κάτω κύψας τῷ δακτύλῳ κατέγραφεν εἰς τὴν γῆν (katō kypsas tō daktylō kategraphen eis tēn gēn, "having stooped down, began writing with a finger on the ground," John 8:6b). Here, as in John 8:8, the remark of Jesus' writing with his finger on the ground is the only reference in the New Testament to Jesus writing anything. This literally enigmatic gesture has been the subject of much conjecture and speculation among scholars. Chris Keith catalogs thirty-eight possibilities to explain what Jesus might have written on the ground.[32] Jerome thinks that Jesus wrote the sins of the woman's accusers on the ground (*Pelag.* 2:17). J. Duncan M. Derrett proposes that Jesus wrote Exodus 23:1b ("You shall not join hands with the wicked" NRSV) in John 8:6b, and Exodus 23:7a ("Keep far from a false charge" NRSV) in John 8:8.[33] Rudolf Schnackenburg suggests that Jesus made a picturesque reference to Jeremiah 17:13 ("Those who turn away from you will be written in the dust because they have forsaken the LORD, the spring of living water" NIV).[34] It is clear that the narrator is only interested in Jesus' gesture of writing, not the content of his writing. At any rate, Jesus' gesture implies either "a studied refusal to pronounce judgement,"[35] or "a sign of indifference, and even disappointment with the proceedings."[36] Note that Jesus' gesture recalls Yahweh's writing the two stone tablets with the finger (Exod 31:18; Deut 9:10).

As the scribes and Pharisees persist in asking him, Jesus straightens up and says to his interlocutors, Ὁ ἀναμάρτητος ὑμῶν πρῶτος ἐπ᾽ αὐτὴν βαλέτω λίθον (Ho anamartētos hymōn prōtos ep' autēn baletō lithon, "The sinless among you let him first cast a stone at her," John 8:7). It is worth

---

32. See Keith, *Pericope Adulterae*, 12–21.

33. See Derrett, *Law in the New Testament*, 175–86.

34. See Schnackenburg, *Gospel According to St. John*, 2:165–66.

35. Barrett, *Gospel According to St. John*, 592.

36. Moloney, *Gospel of John*, 261.

stressing that Jesus' riposte does not endorse violence against the adulteress. On the contrary, it tactfully defends her by appealing to the Mosaic law, which states that witnesses are to cast the first fatal stone, thus signaling to people the beginning process of lapidation (Deut 13:9; 17:7). Since the scribes and Pharisees are unable to produce witnesses, this case must be dismissed. Moreover, his riposte decollectivizes the mob by challenging each one of them to make a personal inventory of his own moral qualification, competence, and motivation before executing a death penalty.[37] The adjective, Ὁ ἀναμάρτητος (Ho anamartētos, "[the one] without sin," John 8:7[38]), means that whoever takes on himself the role of an executioner must have pure motives and must be guiltless before God (Deut 19:16–19; John 8:6a; Rom 2:1). Jesus, whom the scribes and Pharisees have called upon to act as a judge on the applicability of the Mosaic law, turns the table on his interlocutors in a way that does not elicit further religious, legal, and political disputes. The early morning Temple visitors and worshippers are now anxiously guessing what will happen next. Their eyes must be fixed on the mob led by the scribes and Pharisees. They be asking themselves whether the accusers will stone the adulteress to death or not. It will only take one man, and everyone else will jump in.

Having stooped down again, Jesus continues to write on the ground for a second time, thus giving the scribes and Pharisees the space they need to let the full impact of his words deeply reverberate into every fiber of their beings. Unlike the compound verb καταγράφειν (katagraphein[39]), a *hapax legomenon* in the New Testament, used in John 8:6b, the narrator now employs in John 8:8 the simple verb γράφειν (graphein[40]). Both verbs clearly mean "to write" (Exod 32:15 [LXX]). One thing, however, is certain: the narrator wants to emphasize that Jesus was literate.[41]

Upon hearing Jesus' riposte in John 8:7, the scribes and Pharisees ἐξήρχοντο εἷς καθ᾽ εἷς ἀρξάμενοι ἀπὸ τῶν πρεσβυτέρων (exērchonto eis kath eis arxamenoi apo tōn presbyterōn, "went out, one by one, having begun with the elders," John 8:9a). It is worth remarking that those advanced in years are the first to quietly and surreptitiously slip away. All of them have undoubtedly accumulated sins in their personal accounts. Holly J. Toensing correctly

---

37. See Weren, "Use of Violence," 144; Derrett, *Law in the New Testament*, 182.

38. See BDAG, 67.

39. See BDAG, 516.

40. See BDAG, 206–7.

41. See Keith, *Pericope Adulterae*, 257.

remarks, "If the criterion for condemning someone is sinlessness, then the scribes and Pharisees cannot condemn. Their departure signals an honest assessment of themselves and can be understood to be an act of integrity."[42] Moreover, the withdrawal of the woman's accusers signals the dismissal of the case and, consequently, the woman's acquittal.

## Verdict (John 8:9b–11)

Having succeeded in preventing and eliminating the threat of fatal mob violence against the adulteress, Jesus is now left alone with the woman, who has been standing all this time in the middle (ἐν μέσῳ οὖσα, *en mesō ousa*, "being in the middle," John 8:9b; see also John 8:3), and who probably is still surrounded by all the people who have come to listen to Jesus' teaching.

Jesus straightens up, faces her, and asks her two straightforward questions, Γύναι, ποῦ εἰσίν; οὐδείς σε κατέκρινεν (*Gynai, pou eisin; oudeis se katekrinen*, "Woman, where are they? Did no one condemn you?," John 8:10). This is the first time the adulterous woman is directly spoken to in the pericope. The narrator subtly juxtaposes between the attitude and disposition of the scribes and Pharisees, on the one hand, and that of Jesus, on the other hand, toward the adulteress. The former disparagingly reduces her to a passive, silent object on display, while the latter benevolently bestows dignity on her by calling her "woman," which is a courteous way of addressing females (John 2:4; 4:21; 19:26; 20:13, 15). At this juncture, Gail R. O'Day correctly remarks that the verbal parallels between the two scenes of John 8:6b–7b and John 8:8, 10a remarkably show that both the scribes and Pharisees, on the one hand, and the adulterous woman, on the other hand, have received equal treatment from Jesus. She points out that both scenes are composed of four identical verbs, describing Jesus' action and interaction with the accusers and the accused: stoop down (John 8:6a, 8), write on the ground (John 8:6a, 8), straighten up (John 8:7b, 10a), and speak (John 8:7b, 10a).[43]

Jesus' two noncondemnatory questions invite the woman, as a human person, to enter into dialogue with him. She breaks her silence and tells him, Οὐδείς, κύριε (*Hodeis, kyrie*, "No one, sir," John 8:11). In addressing him as κύριε (*kyrie*, "sir," "master," "lord," "Lord"), she respectfully displays reverence for him. Jesus, whose primary concern is to save

---

42. Toensing, "Divine Intervention or Divine Intrusion?," 1:165–66.

43. O'Day, "John 7:53—8:11," 636.

and not to judge (John 3:17; 12:47), replies to her, Οὐδὲ ἐγώ σε κατακρίνω (*Hode egō se katakrinō*, "Neither do I condemn you," John 8:11). Here, as in John 8:10, the compound verb κατακρίνειν (*katakrinein*, "to pronounce a sentence"[44]), a *hapax legomenon* in John's Gospel, describes a judicial verdict involving condemnation and adjudication of punishment. Jesus' liberating words are an acquittal, which enable the traumatized body of the adulterous woman to breathe a deep sigh of relief and gratitude. Jesus finally dismisses her with a stern warning, πορεύου, [καὶ] ἀπὸ τοῦ νῦν μηκέτι ἁμάρτανε (*poreuou, [kai] apo tou nun mēketi hamartane*, "go, [and] from now on sin no more," John 8:11). He sends her away free but commands her to begin a new life devoid of sexual dalliance. Through Jesus, God's compassion and mercy have been extended to the adulteress who "must not fall back into the way that leads to death."[45]

It is worth mentioning at this point that the New Testament pericope of the adulterous woman, as found in John 7:53—8:11, compellingly reminds one of the apocryphal Old Testament story of Susanna, a Greek addition appended to the Hebrew-Aramaic text of Daniel (1–12), now found at Daniel 13 (LXX and Vulg.).[46] In fact, these two narratives share important thematic and verbal parallels, namely, both (1) deal with allegations of adultery; (2) call attention to the accusers' corrupt behavior; (3) highlight the accusers' failure to produce, identify, or locate the paramour; (4) state that both women are condemned and face death by stoning; (5) conclude with both women being rescued by a prophetic figure; and (6) have the compound verbs καταλαμβάνειν (*katalambanein*; Sus 58; John 8:4) and κατακρίνειν (*katakrinein*; Sus 41, 48, 53; John 8:10, 11). However, there remains one fundamental difference between these two narratives: unlike the woman in John, who is presumed guilty of adultery (John 8:3, 4, 11), Susanna is unambiguously innocent (Sus 63).[47]

44. See *BDAG*, 519.

45. Moloney, *Gospel of John*, 264.

46. The story of the two Jewish false and lustful prophets in Babylon, named Ahab and Zedekiah (cf. Jer 29:21–23), who tried to engage in illicit sexual acts with Nebuchadnezzar's daughter and ended up being executed by fire (*b. Sanh.* 93a), recalls the story of Susanna.

47. See further Keith, "Recent and Previous Research," 390–93; Knust and Wasserman, *To Cast the First Stone*, 154–57.

# Bibliography

Achtemeier, Paul J. "'And He Followed Him': Miracles and Discipleship in Mark 10:46–52." *Sem* 11 (1978) 115–45.

———. *Jesus and the Miracle Tradition.* Eugene, OR: Cascade, 2008.

———. *Mark.* Philadelphia: Fortress, 1975.

———. "Toward the Isolation of Pre-Markan Miracle Catenae." *JBL* 89 (1970) 265–91.

Adams, Dwayne H. *The Sinner in Luke.* Eugene, OR: Pickwick, 2008.

Anderson, Gary A. *Sin: A History.* New Haven: Yale University Press, 2009.

Applegate, Judith K. "'And She Wets His Feet with Her Tears': A Feminist Interpretation of Luke 7:36–50." In *Escaping Eden: New Feminist Perspectives on the Bible,* edited by Harold C. Washington et al., 69–90. New York: New York University Press, 1999.

Asiedu-Peprah, Martin. *Johannine Sabbath Conflicts as Juridical Controversy.* Tübingen: Mohr Siebeck, 2001.

Barclay, William. *The Gospel of Luke.* Louisville: Westminster John Knox, 2001.

Barrett, C. K. *The Gospel According to St. John: An Introduction with Commentary and Notes on the Greek Text.* 2nd ed. Philadelphia: Westminster, 1978.

Bauckham, Richard. *Jesus and the Eyewitnesses: The Gospels as Eyewitness Testimony.* 2nd ed. Grand Rapids: Eerdmans, 2017.

Beutler, Johannes. *A Commentary on the Gospel of John.* Translated by Michael Tait. Grand Rapids: Eerdmans, 2017.

Bird, Michael F. *The Gospel of the Lord. How the Early Church Wrote the Story of Jesus.* Grand Rapids: Eerdmans, 2014.

———. *Jesus and the Origins of the Gentile Mission.* New York: T. & T. Clark International, 2006.

Blackburn, Barry. *Theios Anēr and the Markan Miracle Traditions: A Critique of the Theios Anēr Concept as an Interpretative Background of the Miracle Traditions Used by Mark.* Tübingen: Mohr Siebeck, 1991.

Boadt, Lawrence. *Reading the Old Testament: An Introduction.* New York: Paulist, 1984.

Bock, Darrell L. *Luke, Volume 1: 1:1—9:50.* Grand Rapids: Baker, 1994.

———. *Luke, Volume 2: 9:51—24:53.* Grand Rapids: Baker, 1996.

Borchert, Gerald L. *John 1–11.* Nashville: Broadman & Holman, 1996.

Borgen, Peder. *Early Christianity and Hellenistic Judaism.* Edinburgh: T. & T. Clark, 1996.

Bovon, François. *Luke 1: A Commentary on the Gospel of Luke 1:1—9:50.* Translated by Christine M. Thomas. Minneapolis: Fortress, 2002.

———. *Luke 2: A Commentary on the Gospel of Luke 9:51—19:27*. Translated by Donald S. Deer. Minneapolis: Fortress, 2013.

Brown, Raymond E. *The Gospel According to John (I–XII): Introduction, Translation, and Notes*. Garden City, NY: Doubleday, 1966.

———. *An Introduction to the New Testament*. New York: Doubleday, 1997.

Bruehler, Bart B. *A Public and Political Christ: The Social-Spatial Characteristics of Luke 18:35—19:48 and the Gospel as a Whole in Its Ancient Context*. Eugene, OR: Pickwick, 2011.

Bultmann, Rudolf. *The Gospel of John: A Commentary*. Translated by G. R. Beasley-Murray et al. Philadelphia: Westminster, 1971.

———. *The History of the Synoptic Tradition*. Translated by John Marsh. Oxford: Basil Blackwell, 1963.

———. *Theology of the New Testament*. Translated by Kendrick Grobel. Waco, TX: Baylor University Press, 2007.

Burge, Gary M. "Siloam, Bethesda, and the Johannine Water Motif." In *Jesus, John, and History, Volume 3: Glimpses of Jesus through the Johannine Lens*, edited by Paul N. Anderson et al., 3:259–69. Atlanta: SBL, 2016.

Burridge, Richard A. *Four Gospels, One Jesus? A Symbolic Reading*. Grand Rapids: Eerdmans, 2014.

Cadbury, Henry J. "A Possible Case of Lukan Authorship (John 7:53—8:11)." *HTR* 10 (1917) 237–44.

Calduch-Benages, Nuria. *The Perfume of the Gospel: Jesus' Encounters with Women*. Translated by Pascale-Dominique Nau. Rome: Gregorian and Biblical, 2012.

Carroll, John T. *Luke: A Commentary*. Louisville: Westminster John Knox, 2012.

Carson, D. A. *The Gospel According to John*. Grand Rapids: Eerdmans, 1991.

Catchpole, David. *The Quest for Q*. London: Bloomsbury, 2015.

Charlesworth, James H. *Jesus as Mirrored in John: The Genius in the New Testament*. London: T. & T. Clark, 2019.

———. "The Son of David: Solomon and Jesus (Mark 10:47)." In *The New Testament and Hellenistic Judaism*, edited by Peder Borgen et al., 72–87. Peabody, MA: Hendrickson, 1997.

Chilton, Bruce. "Amen." In *ABD* 1:184–86.

Coakley, J. F. "The Anointing at Bethany and the Priority of John." *JBL* 107 (1988) 241–56.

Cohen, Shaye J. D. *From the Maccabees to the Mishnah*. Louisville: Westminster John Knox, 1987.

Collins, Adele Y. *Mark: A Commentary*. Minneapolis: Fortress, 2007.

———. "The Origin of the Designation of Jesus as 'Son of Man.'" *HTR* 80 (1987) 391–407.

Corbo, Virgilio C. "Capernaum." In *ABD* 1:866–68.

Corley, Kathleen E. *Private Women, Public Meals: Social Conflict in the Synoptic Tradition*. Peabody, MA: Hendrickson, 1993.

Cosgrove, Charles H. "The Divine Δεῖ in Luke-Acts: Investigations into the Lukan Understanding of God's Providence." *NovT* 26 (1984) 168–90.

———. "A Woman's Unbound Hair in the Greco-Roman World, with Special Reference to the Story of the 'Sinful Woman' in Luke 7:36–50." *JBL* 124 (2005) 675–92.

Cranfield, C. E. B. *The Gospel According to St. Mark: An Introduction and Commentary*. Cambridge: Cambridge University Press, 1959.

Cullmann, Oscar. *The Christology of the New Testament*. Translated by Shirley C. Guthrie et al. Philadelphia: Westminster, 1963.

Culpepper, R. Alan. *The Gospel and Letters of John*. Nashville: Abingdon, 1998.

———. "Mark 10:50: Why Mention the Garment?" *JBL* 101 (1982) 131–32.

Davies, W. D., and Dale C. Allison. *A Critical and Exegetical Commentary on the Gospel According to Saint Matthew. Volume II: Commentary on Matthew VIII-XVIII*. London: T. & T. Clark International, 1991.

Denaux, Adelbert. *Studies in the Gospel of Luke: Structure, Language and Theology*. Berlin: LIT, 2010.

Derrett, J. Duncan M. *Law in the New Testament*. 1970. Reprint, Eugene, OR: Wipf & Stock, 2005.

———. "Law in the New Testament: The Syro-Phoenician Woman and the Centurion of Capernaum." *NovT* 15 (1973) 161–86.

———. "Mark's Technique: the Haemorrhaging Woman and Jairus' Daughter." *Bib* 63 (1982) 474–505.

Dewey, Joanna. *Markan Public Debate: Literary Technique, Concentric Structure, and Theology in Mark 2:1—3:6*. Chico, CA: Scholars, 1980.

Dibelius, Martin. *From Tradition to Gospel*. Translated by Bertram Lee Woolf. Cambridge: James Clarke, 1971.

Dodd, C. H. *Historical Tradition in the Fourth Gospel*. Cambridge: Cambridge University Press, 1963.

Donahue, John R. *Are You the Christ? The Trial Narrative in the Gospel of Mark*. Missoula, MT: Scholars, 1973.

———. "Recent Studies on the Origin of 'Son of Man' in the Gospels." *CBQ* 48 (1986) 484–98.

———. "Tax Collectors and Sinners: An Attempt at Identification." *CBQ* 33 (1971) 39–61.

Donahue, John R., and Daniel J. Harrington. *The Gospel of Mark*. Collegeville, MN: Liturgical, 2002.

Dunn, James D. G. *Jesus, Paul, and the Law: Studies in Mark and Galatians*. Louisville: Westminster John Knox, 1990.

———. *Jesus Remembered: Christianity in the Making*. Volume 1. Grand Rapids: Eerdmans, 2003.

Edwards, James R. *The Gospel According to Luke*. Grand Rapids: Eerdmans, 2015.

———. *The Gospel According to Mark*. Grand Rapids: Eerdmans, 2002.

———. *The Hebrew Gospel and the Development of Synoptic Tradition*. Grand Rapids: Eerdmans, 2009.

———. "Markan Sandwiches: The Significance of Interpolations in Markan Narratives." *NovT* 31 (1989) 193–216.

Elliott, J. K. "The Anointing of Jesus." *ExpTim* 85 (1974) 105–7.

Ellis, E. Earle. *The Gospel of Luke*. 1983. Reprint, Eugene, OR: Wipf & Stock, 2003.

Evans, Craig. A. *Matthew*. Cambridge: Cambridge University Press, 2012.

Eve, Eric. *The Jewish Context of Jesus' Miracles*. London: Sheffield, 2002.

Fee, Gordon D. "On the Inauthenticity of John 5:3b–4." *EvQ* 54 (1982) 207–18.

Fitzmyer, Joseph A. *The Gospel According to Luke (I-IX): Introduction, Translation, and Notes*. Garden City, NY: Doubleday, 1981.

———. *The Gospel According to Luke (X-XXIV): Introduction, Translation, and Notes*. Garden City, NY: Doubleday, 1985.

———. *A Wandering Aramean: Collected Aramaic Essays*. Missoula, MT: Scholars, 1979.

Fleddermann, Harry T. *Q: A Reconstruction and Commentary*. Leuven: Peetres, 2005.

Focant, Camille. *The Gospel According to Mark: A Commentary*. Translated by Leslie Robert Keylock. Eugene, OR: Pickwick, 2012.

Fowler, Robert M. *Let the Reader Understand. Reader-Response Criticism and the Gospel of Mark*. Harrisburg, PA: Trinity, 1996.

France, R. T. "Exegesis in Practice: Two Samples." In *New Testament Interpretation: Essays on Principles and Methods*, edited by I. Howard Marshall, 252–81. 1977. Reprint, Eugene, OR: Wipf & Stock, 2006.

———. *The Gospel of Mark. A Commentary on the Greek Text*. Grand Rapids: Eerdmans, 2002.

———. *The Gospel of Matthew*. Grand Rapids: Eerdmans, 2007.

Gagnon, Robert A. J. "Luke's Motives for Redaction in the Account of the Double Delegation in Luke 7:1–10." *NovT* 36 (1994) 122–45.

———. "The Shape of Matthew's Q Text of the Centurion at Capernaum: Did It Mention Delegations?" *NTS* 40 (1994) 133–42.

———. "Statistical Analysis and the Case of the Double Delegation in Luke 7:3–7a." *CBQ* 55 (1993) 709–31.

Gill, David. "Observations on the Lukan Travel Narrative and Some Related Passages." *HTR* 63 (1970) 199–221.

Godet, Frédéric L. *A Commentary on the Gospel of St. Luke*. Translated by E. W. Shalders et al. New York: Funk, 1881.

Gowler, David B. *Host, Guest, Enemy and Friend: Portraits of the Pharisees in Luke and Acts*. New York: Lang, 1991.

Green, Elizabeth E. "Making Her Case and Reading It Too: Feminist Readings of the Story of the Woman Taken in Adultery." In *Ciphers in the Sand: Interpretations of The Woman Taken in Adultery (John 7:53—8:11)*, edited by Larry J. Kreitzer et al., 240–67. Sheffield: Sheffield, 2000.

Green, Joel B. *The Gospel of Luke*. Grand Rapids: Eerdmans, 1997.

———. *The Way of the Cross: Following Jesus in the Gospel of Mark*. Eugene, OR: Wipf & Stock, 2009.

Guelich, Robert A. *Mark 1—8:26*. Dallas: Word, 1989.

Gundry, Robert H. *Mark: A Commentary on His Apology for the Cross, Volume 1 (1–8)*. Grand Rapids: Eerdmans, 1993.

———. *Mark: A Commentary on His Apology for the Cross, Volume 2 (9–16)*. Grand Rapids: Eerdmans, 1993.

———. *Matthew: A Commentary on His Handbook for a Mixed Church under Persecution*. 2nd ed. Grand Rapids: Eerdmans, 1994.

Haenchen, Ernst. *John 1: A Commentary on the Gospel of John Chapters 1–6*. Translated by Robert W. Funk. Philadelphia: Fortress, 1984.

Hägerland, Tobias. *Jesus and the Forgiveness of Sins: An Aspect of His Prophetic Mission*. Cambridge: Cambridge University Press, 2011.

Hamm, Dennis. "Luke 19:8 Once Again: Does Zacchaeus Defend or Resolve?" *JBL* 107 (1988) 431–37.

———. "Zacchaeus Revisited Once More: A Story of Vindication or Conversion?" *Bib* 72 (1991) 249–52.

Harrington, Daniel J. *The Gospel of Matthew*. Collegeville, MN: Liturgical, 1991.

Harris, Sarah. *The Davidic Shepherd King in the Lukan Narrative*. London: T. & T. Clark, 2016.

Heil, John P. "The Story of Jesus and the Adulteress (John 7,53—8,11) Reconsidered." *Bib* 72 (1991) 182–91.

Holland, T. A., and Ehud Netzer. "Jericho." In *ABD* 3:723–40.

Holst, Robert. "The One Anointing of Jesus: Another Application of the Form-Critical Method." *JBL* 95 (1976) 435–46.

Hooker, Morna D. *A Commentary on the Gospel According to St. Mark.* London: Continuum, 1991.

Hornsby, Teresa J. "Why Is She Crying? A Feminist Interpretation of Luke 7:36–50." In *Escaping Eden: New Feminist Perspectives on the Bible,* edited by Harold C. Washington et al., 91–103. New York: New York University Press, 1999.

Hultgren, Arland J. *Jesus and His Adversaries: The Form and Function of the Conflict Stories in the Synoptic Tradition.* Minneapolis: Augsburg, 1979.

———. *The Parables of Jesus: A Commentary.* Grand Rapids: Eerdmans, 2000.

Iersel, Bas M. F. van. *Mark: A Reader-Response Commentary.* Translated by W. H. Bisscheroux. Sheffield: Sheffield, 1998.

Ireland, Dennis J. *Stewardship and the Kingdom of God: An Historical, Exegetical, and Contextual Study of the Parable of the Unjust Steward in Luke 16:1–13.* Leiden: Brill, 1992.

Jeremias, Joachim. *Jerusalem in the Time of Jesus: An Investigation into Economic and Social Conditions during the New Testament Period.* Translated by F. H. Cave et al. Philadelphia: Fortress, 1975.

Jipp, Joshua W. *Divine Visitations and Hospitality to Strangers in Luke-Acts: An Interpretation of the Malta Episode in Acts 28:1–10.* Leiden: Brill, 2013.

Johnson, Earl S. "Mark 10:46–52: Blind Bartimaeus." *CBQ* 40 (1978) 191–204.

Johnson, Luke Timothy. *The Gospel of Luke.* Collegeville, MN: Liturgical, 1991.

———. *The Writings of the New Testament: An Interpretation.* London: SCM, 1999.

Just, Arthur A. *The Ongoing Feast: Table Fellowship and Eschatology at Emmaus.* Collegeville, MN: Liturgical, 1993.

Karris, Robert J. *Eating Your Way through Luke's Gospel.* Collegeville, MN: Liturgical, 2006.

Keener, Craig S. *The Gospel of John: A Commentary.* Volume 1. Peabody, MA: Hendrickson, 2003.

———. *The Gospel of Matthew: A Socio-Rhetorical Commentary.* Grand Rapids: Eerdmans, 2009.

Keith, Chris. *The Pericope Adulterae, the Gospel of John, and the Literacy of Jesus.* Leiden: Brill, 2009.

———. "Recent and Previous Research on the Pericope Adulterae (John 7.53—8.11)." *CBR* 6 (2008) 377–404.

Kelber, Werner H. *Mark's Story of Jesus.* Philadelphia: Fortress, 1979.

Kelso, James L. "New Testament Jericho." *BA* 14 (1951) 34–43.

Kilgallen, John J. "Faith and Forgiveness: Luke 7,36–50." *RB* 112 (2005) 372–84.

———. "Forgiveness of Sins (Luke 7:36–50)." *NovT* 40 (1998) 105–16.

———. "A Proposal for Interpreting Luke 7,36–50." *Bib* 72 (1991) 305–30.

Kingsbury, Jack Dean. "The Title 'Kyrios' in Matthew's Gospel." *JBL* 94 (1975) 246–55.

Kinman, Brent. *Jesus' Entry into Jerusalem: In the Context of Lukan Theology and the Politics of His Day.* Leiden: Brill, 1995.

Kinukawa, Hisako. "On John 7:53—8:11: A Well-Cherished but Much-Clouded Story." In *Reading from this Place: Social Location and Biblical Interpretation in Global Perspective,* edited by Fernando F. Segovia et al., 82–96. Volume 2. Minneapolis: Fortress, 1995.

Kloppenborg, John S. *Excavating Q: The History and Setting of the Sayings Gospel.* Minneapolis: Fortress, 2000.

―――. *The Formation of Q: Trajectories in Ancient Wisdom Collections.* Harrisburg, PA: Trinity, 1999.

―――. *Q, the Earliest Gospel: An Introduction to the Original Stories and Sayings of Jesus.* Louisville: Westminster John Knox, 2008.

Knox, Wilfred L. *The Sources of the Synoptic Gospels. Volume 2: St. Luke and St. Matthew.* Cambridge: Cambridge University Press, 1957.

Knust, Jennifer, and Tommy Wasserman. *To Cast the First Stone: The Transmission of a Gospel Story.* Princeton: Princeton University Press, 2018.

Kok, Jacobus. *New Perspectives on Healing, Restoration and Reconciliation in John's Gospel.* Leiden: Brill, 2017.

Köstenberger, Andreas J. "A Comparison of the Pericopae of Jesus' Anointing." In *Studies in John and Gender: A Decade of Scholarship*, by Andreas J. Köstenberger, 49–63. New York: Lang, 2001.

―――. *John.* Grand Rapids: Baker, 2004.

Kysar, Robert. *John: The Maverick Gospel.* 3rd ed. Louisville: Westminster John Knox, 1993.

―――. *Voyages with John: Charting the Fourth Gospel.* Waco, TX: Baylor University Press, 2005.

Lachs, Samuel Tobias. "Studies in the Semitic Background to the Gospel of Matthew." *JQR* 67 (1977) 195–217.

Lane, William L. *The Gospel According to Mark: The English Text with Introduction, Exposition, and Notes.* Grand Rapids: Eerdmans, 1974.

LaVerdiere, Eugene. *Dining in the Kingdom of God: The Origins of the Eucharist in the Gospel of Luke.* Chicago: Liturgy Training, 1994.

Legault, André. "An Application of the Form-Critique Method to the Anointings in Galilee (Lk. 7, 36–50) and Bethany (Mt. 26, 6–13; Mk. 14, 3–9; Jn. 12, 1–8)." *CBQ* 16 (1954) 131–45.

Levine, Amy-Jill. "Matthew's Advice to a Divided Readership." In *The Gospel of Matthew in Current Study*, edited by D. E. Aune, 22–41. Grand Rapids: Eerdmans, 2001.

Levine, Amy-Jill, and Ben Witherington. *The Gospel of Luke.* Cambridge: Cambridge University Press, 2018.

Lightfoot, R. H. *St. John's Gospel: A Commentary*, edited by C. F. Evans. Oxford: Clarendon, 1957.

Loewe, William P. "Towards an Interpretation of Lk 19:1–10." *CBQ* 36 (1974) 321–31.

Loos, H. van der. *Miracles of Jesus.* Leiden: Brill, 1965.

Luz, Ulrich. *Matthew 8–20: A Commentary.* Translated by James E. Crouch. Minneapolis: Fortress, 2001.

Maccini, Robert Gordon. *Her Testimony Is True: Women as Witnesses According to John.* Sheffield: Sheffield, 1996.

Maccoby, Hyam. *Ritual and Morality: The Ritual Purity System and Its Place in Judaism.* Cambridge: Cambridge University Press, 1999.

Malbon, Elizabeth Struthers. *Hearing Mark: A Listener's Guide.* Harrisburg, PA: Trinity, 2002.

―――. *In the Company of Jesus: Characters in Mark's Gospel.* Louisville: Westminster John Knox, 2000.

Marcus, Joel. *Mark 1–8: A New Translation with Introduction and Commentary*. New York: Doubleday, 2000.

———. *Mark 8–16: A New Translation with Introduction and Commentary*. Binghamton, NY: Yale University Press, 2009.

———. *The Way of the Lord. Christological Exegesis of the Old Testament in the Gospel of Mark*. Louisville: Westminster Knox, 1992.

Marshall, Christopher D. *Faith as a Theme in Mark's Narrative*. Cambridge: Cambridge University Press, 1989.

Marshall, I. Howard. *The Gospel of Luke*. Grand Rapids: Paternoster, 1978.

———. "The Synoptic 'Son of Man' Sayings in the Light of Linguistic Studies." In *The Son of Man Problem: Critical Reading*, edited by B. E. Reynolds, 132–50. New York: T. & T. Clark, 2018.

Matera, Frank J. "Jesus' Journey to Jerusalem (Luke 9:51—19:46): A Conflict with Israel." *JSNT* 51 (1993) 57–77.

McNamara, Martin. *Targum and Testament Revisited: Aramaic Paraphrases of the Hebrew Bible: A Light on the New Testament*. 2nd ed. Grand Rapids: Eerdmans, 2010.

McNeile, Alan Hugh. *The Gospel According to St. Matthew: The Greek Text, with Introduction, Notes, and Indices*. London: Macmillan, 1915.

Meier, John P. *A Marginal Jew. Rethinking the Historical Jesus. Mentor, Message, and Miracles*. Volume 2. New York: Doubleday, 1994.

———. *Matthew*. Collegeville, MN: Liturgical, 1980.

Mendez-Moratalla, Fernando. *The Paradigm of Conversion in Luke*. London: T. & T. Clark International, 2004.

Menken, Maarten J. J. "The Call of Blind Bartimaeus (Mark 10:46–52)." *HvTSt* 61 (2005) 273–90. https://hts.org.za/index.php/hts/article/view/442/341.

Metzger, Bruce M. *A Textual Commentary on the Greek New Testament*. 2nd ed. Stuttgart: Deutsche Bibelgesellschaft, 1971.

Metzger, Bruce M., and Bart Ehrman. *The Text of the New Testament: Its Transmission, Corruption, and Restoration*. Oxford: Oxford University Press, 2005.

Metzger, James A. *Consumption and Wealth in Luke's Travel Narrative*. Leiden: Brill, 2007.

Michaels, J. Ramsey. *The Gospel of John*. Grand Rapids: Eerdmans, 2010.

Miller, Susan. *Women in Mark's Gospel*. London: T. & T. Clark International, 2004.

Mitchell, Alan C. "The Use of συκοφαντεῖν in Luke 19,8: Further Evidence for Zacchaeus's Defense." *Bib* 72 (1991) 546–47.

———. "Zacchaeus Revisited: Luke 19,8 as a Defense." *Bib* 71 (1990) 153–76.

Moloney, Francis J. *The Gospel of John*. Collegeville, MN: Liturgical, 1998.

———. *The Gospel of Mark: A Commentary*. Peabody, MA: Hendrickson, 2002.

Morris, Leon. *The Gospel According to Matthew*. Grand Rapids: Eerdmans, 1992.

Moule, C. F. D. *An Idiom Book of New Testament Greek*. Cambridge: Cambridge University Press, 1953.

———. *The Origin of Christology*. Cambridge: Cambridge University Press, 1977.

Mullen, J. Patrick. *Dining with Pharisees*. Collegeville, MN: Liturgical, 2004.

Murphy-O'Connor, Jerome. *The Holy Land: An Oxford Archaeological Guide from Earliest Times to 1700*. Oxford: Oxford University Press, 2008.

———. *Keys to Jerusalem: Collected Essays*. Oxford: Oxford University Press, 2012.

Neirynck, Frans. *Duality in Mark: Contributions to the Study of the Markan Redaction*. Leuven: Leuven University Press, 1988.

———. "Synoptic Problem." In *NJBC* 40:587–95.

Neusner, Jacob. *A Rabbi Talks with Jesus.* Montreal: McGill-Queen University Press, 2000.

———. "The Religious Meaning of Bodily Excretions in Rabbinic Judaism: The Halakhah on Leviticus Chapter Fifteen: Zabim and Niddah." In *The Annual of Rabbinic Judaism: Ancient, Medieval, and Modern,* edited by Alan J. Avery-Peck et al., 67–91. Volume 3. Leiden: Brill, 2000.

Nicol, W. *The Sēmeia in the Fourth Gospel: Tradition and Redaction.* Leiden: Brill, 1972.

Nolland, John. *The Gospel of Matthew: A Commentary on the Greek Text.* Grand Rapids: Eerdmans, 2005.

———. *Luke 18:35—24:43.* Dallas: Word, 1993.

O'Collins, Gerald. *Rethinking Fundamental Theology: Toward A New Fundamental Theology.* Oxford: Oxford University Press, 2011.

O'Day, Gail R. "John 7:53—8:11: A Study in Misreading." *JBL* 111 (1992) 631–40.

O'Day, Gail R., and Susan Hylen. *John.* Louisville: Westminster John Knox, 2006.

Ó Fearghail, Fearghus. *The Introduction to Luke-Acts: A Study of the Role of Lk 1, 1–4, 44 in the Composition of Luke's Two-Volume Work.* Roma: Pontificio Istituto Biblico, 1991.

O'Hanlon, John. "The Story of Zacchaeus and the Lukan Ethic." *JSNT* 12 (1981) 2–26.

Osborne, Grant R. *Matthew.* Grand Rapids: Zondervan, 2010.

Ossandón, Juan Carlos. "Bartimaeus' Faith: Plot and Point of View in Mark 10,46–52." *Bib* 93 (2012) 377–402.

O'Toole, Robert F. "The Literary Form of Luke 19:1–10." *JBL* 110 (1991) 107–16.

———. *Luke's Presentation of Jesus: A Christology.* Roma: Pontificio Istituto Biblico, 2004.

Paffenroth, Kim. *The Story of Jesus According to Luke.* Sheffield: Sheffield, 1997.

Parsons, Mikeal C. "'Short in Stature': Luke's Physical Description of Zacchaeus." *NTS* 47 (2001) 50–57.

Perkins, Pheme. "The Gospel According to John." In *NJBC* 61:942–85.

———. "Taxes in the New Testament." *JRE* 12 (1984) 182–200.

Perrin, Norman. *The New Testament: An Introduction. Proclamation and Parenesis, Myth and History.* New York: Harcourt Brace Jovanovich, 1974.

———. *What Is Redaction Criticism?* Philadelphia: Fortress, 1969.

Petersen, William L. "ΟΥΔΕ ΕΓΩ ΣΕ [ΚΑΤΑ]ΚΡΙΝΩ. John 8:11, the *Protevangilum Iacobi,* and the History of the *Pericope Adulterae.*" In *Sayings of Jesus: Canonical and Non-canonical: Essays in Honor of Tjitze Baarda,* edited by William L. Petersen et al., 191–221. Leiden: Brill, 1997.

Plummer, Alfred. *A Critical and Exegetical Commentary on the Gospel According to St. Luke.* New York: Scribner's Sons, 1902.

Punch, John David. "The Piously Offensive Pericope Adulterae." In *The Pericope of the Adulteress in Contemporary Research,* edited by David Alan Black et al., 7–31. London: Bloomsbury T. & T. Clark, 2016.

Ravens, D. A. S. "Zacchaeus : The Final Part of a Lucan Triptych?" *JSNT* 41 (1991) 19–32.

Reed, Jonathan L. *Archaeology and the Galilean Jesus: A Re-examination of Evidence.* Harrisburg, PA: Trinity, 2000.

Reid, Barbara E. *Choosing the Better Part? Women in the Gospel of Luke.* Collegeville, MN: Liturgical, 1996.

Rengstorf, K. H. "ἱκανός, ἱκανότης, ἱκανόω." In *TDNT* 3:293–96.

Rhoads, David M., et al. *Mark as Story. An Introduction to the Narrative of a Gospel.* Minneapolis: Fortress, 1999.

Ridderbos, Herman. *The Gospel of John: A Theological Commentary.* Translated by John Vriend. Grand Rapids: Eerdmans, 1997.

Robbins, Vernon K. "The Healing of Blind Bartimaeus (10:46–52) in the Marcan Theology." *JBL* 92 (1973) 224–42.

———. "The Woman Who Touched Jesus' Garment: Socio-Rhetorical Analysis of the Synoptic Accounts." *NTS* 33 (1987) 502–15.

Robertson, A. T. *A Grammar of the Greek New Testament in the Light of Historical Research.* New York: Hodder & Stoughton, 1923.

Robinson, William C. "The Theological Context for Interpreting Luke's Travel Narrative (9:51 ff.)." *JBL* 79 (1960) 20–31.

Rousseau, John J., and Rami Arav. *Jesus and His World: An Archaeological and Cultural Dictionary.* Minneapolis, Fortress, 1995.

Safrai, Shmuel. "The Synagogue the Centurion Built." *JP* 55 (1998) 12–14.

Sanders, E. P. *The Historical Figure of Jesus.* London: Penguin, 1995.

———. *Jesus and Judaism.* London: SCM, 1985.

———. *Judaism: Practice and Belief, 63 BCE–66 CE.* Minneapolis: Fortress, 2016.

Schnackenburg, Rudolf. *The Gospel According to St. John. Volume 2: Commentary on Chapters 5–12.* Translated by Cecily Hastings et al. New York: Crossroad, 1980.

———. *The Gospel of Matthew.* Translated by Robert R. Barr. Grand Rapids: Eerdmans, 2002.

Schürer, Emil. *The History of the Jewish People in the Age of Jesus Christ (175 B.C.–A.D. 135).* Volume 1. Edited by Geza Vermes et al. Edinburgh: T. & T. Clark, 1973.

Schweizer, Eduard. *The Good News According to Luke.* Translated by David E. Green. Atlanta: John Knox, 1984.

———. *The Good News According to Mark.* Translated by Donald H. Madvig. Atlanta: John Knox, 1970.

———. *The Good News According to Matthew.* Translated by David E. Green. Atlanta: John Knox, 1975.

Selvidge, Marla J. "Mark 5:25–34 and Leviticus 15:19–20: A Reaction to Restrictive Purity Regulations." *JBL* 103 (1984) 619–23.

Senior, Donald. "Between Two Worlds: Gentiles and Jewish Christians in Matthew's Gospel." *CBQ* 61 (1999) 1–23.

———. *The Passion of Jesus in the Gospel of Mark.* Collegeville, MN: Liturgical, 1984.

Shepherd, Tom. "The Narrative Function of Markan Intercalation." *NTS* 41 (1995) 522–40.

Siegman, Edward F. "St. John's Use of the Synoptic Material." *CBQ* 30 (1968) 182–98.

Siker, Jeffery S. *Disinheriting the Jews: Abraham in Early Christian Controversy.* Louisville: Westminster John Knox, 1991.

Skinner, John E. *The Christian Disciple.* Lanham, MD: University Press of America, 1984.

Smith, Dennis E. *From Symposium to Eucharist: The Banquet in the Early Christian World.* Minneapolis: Fortress, 2003.

Smith, D. Moody. *The Composition and Order of the Fourth Gospel: Bultmann's Literary Theory.* New Haven: Yale University Press, 1965.

———. *Johannine Christianity: Essays on Its Setting, Sources and Theology.* Columbia: University of South Carolina Press, 1984.

Steele, E. Springs. "Luke 11:37–54: A Modified Hellenistic Symposium?" *JBL* 103 (1984) 379–94.

Stein, Robert H. *Luke.* Nashville: B & H, 1992.

———. *Mark.* Grand Rapids: Baker, 2008.

Steinhauser, Michael G. "The Form of the Bartimaeus Narrative (Mark 10.46–52)." *NTS* 32 (1986) 583–95.

————. "Part of a 'Call Story'?" *ExpTim* 94 (1983) 204–6.

Strauss, Mark L. *Four Portraits, One Jesus: A Survey of Jesus and the Gospels*. Grand Rapids: Zondervan, 2007.

Streeter, Burnett Hillman. *The Four Gospels: A Study of Origins, Treating of the Manuscript Tradition, Sources, Authorship, and Dates*. London: Macmillan, 1924.

Talbert, Charles H. *Matthew*. Grand Rapids: Baker, 2010.

————. *Reading Luke: A Literary and Theological Commentary on the Third Gospel*. New York: Crossroad, 1982.

Tannehill, Robert C. *Luke*. Nashville: Abingdon, 1996.

————. *The Shape of Luke's Story: Essays on Luke-Acts*. Eugene, OR: Cascade, 2005.

Taylor, Vincent. *The Formation of the Gospel Tradition*. London: Macmillan, 1933.

————. *The Gospel According to St. Mark: The Greek Text with Introduction, Notes, and Indices*. London: Macmillan, 1955.

Theissen, Gerd. *The Gospels in Context: Social and Political History in the Synoptic Tradition*. Translated by Linda M. Maloney. Edinburgh: T. & T. Clark, 1992.

————. *The Miracle Stories of the Early Christian Tradition*. Translated by Francis McDonagh. Philadelphia: Fortress, 1983.

————. *The Shadow of the Galilean: The Quest of the Historical Jesus in Narrative Form*. Translated by John Bowden. Philadelphia: Fortress, 1987.

Theissen, Gerd, and Annette Merz. *The Historical Jesus: A Comprehensive Guide*. Translated by John Bowden. Minneapolis: Fortress, 1998.

Thomas, Esposite. *Jesus' Meals with Pharisees and their Liturgical Roots*. Rome: Gregorian and Biblical, 2015.

Toensing, Holly J. "Divine Intervention or Divine Intrusion? Jesus and the Adulteress in John's Gospel." In *A Feminist Companion to John*, edited by Amy-Jill Levine, 159–72. Volume 1. Sheffield: Sheffield, 2003.

Tuckett, Christopher M. *Q and the History of Early Christianity: Studies on Q*. London: T. & T. Clark International, 2004.

————. "Synoptic Problem." In *ABD* 6:263–70.

Varghese, Johns. *The Imagery of Love in the Gospel of John*. Rome: Gregorian and Biblical, 2009.

Vassiliadis, Petros. "The Nature and Extent of the Q-Document." *NovT* 20 (1978) 49–73.

Vermes, Geza. *The Complete Dead Sea Scrolls in English*. Minneapolis: Fortress, 1962.

————. *Jesus the Jew: A Historian's Reading of the Gospels*. London: SCM, 1994.

Wahlde, U. C. von. "Archaeology and John's Gospel." In *Jesus and Archaeology*, edited by James H. Charlesworth, 523–86. Grand Rapids: Eerdmans, 2006.

Walaskay, Paul W. *'And so We Came to Rome': The Political Perspective of St. Luke*. Cambridge: Cambridge University Press, 1983.

Wallace, Daniel B. "Reconsidering 'The Story of Jesus and the Adulteress Woman Reconsidered.'" *NTS* 39 (1993) 290–96.

Weiss, Herold. "The Sabbath in the Fourth Gospel." *JBL* 110 (1991) 311–21.

Weren, Wim J. C. "The Use of Violence in Punishing Adultery in Biblical Texts (Deuteronomy 22:13–29 and John 7:53—8:11)." In *Coping with Violence in the New Testament*, edited by Pieter G. R. de Villiers et al., 133–50. Leiden: Brill, 2012.

White, Richard C. "Vindication for Zacchaeus?" *ExpTim* 91 (1979) 21.

Williams, Joel. *Other Followers of Jesus: Minor Characters as Major Figures in Mark's Gospel*. Sheffield: Sheffield, 1994.

Witherington, Ben. *John's Wisdom: A Commentary on the Fourth Gospel.* Louisville: Westminster John Knox, 1995.

———. *Women and the Genesis of Christianity.* Cambridge: Cambridge University Press, 1990.

———. *Women in the Ministry of Jesus: A Study of Jesus' Attitude to Women and their Roles as Reflected in His Earthly Life.* Cambridge: Cambridge University Press, 1984.

Wright, Benjamin G., and Claudia V. Camp. "'Who Has Been Tested By Gold and Found Perfect?' Ben Sira's Discourse of Riches and Poverty." In *Praise Israel for Wisdom and Instruction: Essays on Ben Sira and Wisdom, the Letter of Aristeas and the Septuagint,* edited by Benjamin G. Wright, 71–96. Leiden: Brill, 2008.

Yamasaki, Gary. "Point of View in a Gospel Story: What Difference Does It Make? Luke 19:1–10 as a Test Case." *JBL* 125 (2006) 89–105.

York, John. *The Last Shall Be First: The Rhetoric of Reversal in Luke.* London: Bloomsbury, 2015.

# Ancient Document Index

# Hebrew Bible/Old Testament Apocrypha and Pseudepigrapha